When Your Fairy Tale Fails

*How I Survived the Devastation of
My Spouse's Sexual Addiction*

KRISTEN MICHAELS

WESTBOW
PRESS®
A DIVISION OF THOMAS NELSON
& ZONDERVAN

This book is a work of non-fiction. Unless otherwise noted, the author and the publisher
make no explicit guarantees as to the accuracy of the information contained in this book
and in some cases, names of people and places have been altered to protect their privacy.

WestBow Press books may be ordered through booksellers or by contacting:

WestBow Press
A Division of Thomas Nelson & Zondervan
1663 Liberty Drive
Bloomington, IN 47403
www.westbowpress.com
844-714-3454

ISBN: 978-1-6642-3921-0 (sc)
ISBN: 978-1-6642-3920-3 (hc)
ISBN: 978-1-6642-3922-7 (e)

Library of Congress Control Number: 2021913368

Print information available on the last page.

WestBow Press rev. date: 08/06/2021

Contents

Introduction:
This is BS

HEN I FIRST FOUND OUT ABOUT MY HUSBAND'S SEXUAL addiction, a cocktail of surreal confusion, panic, and pain disoriented me in a way I had never experienced. I searched the web laboriously, looking for answers as to what was happening to me and why. I remember seeing the initials BS scattered throughout so many chat rooms and blog posts. I read the posts, trying to figure out what it stood for, and finally found an article that defined it as "betrayed spouse." Even in my devastation and in the midst of the gut-wrenching, painstaking climb toward healthiness, I couldn't help but snicker at the abbreviation. I hate many of the terms associated with sexual addiction, like *acting out*, but this one fit. I mean that in the more typical sense of the abbreviation. You don't deserve this. You didn't cause this. Even so, here you are, and there I was just a short time ago.

You have been hurt. As unfair as it is, it is your job to heal from that hurt; it is not your spouse's job to fix your hurt for you. Dr. Henry Cloud explains this by saying that if someone comes up to you and breaks your legs, it is their fault, but you are still the one that has to go to the hospital, complete physical therapy, and experience the pain as the wounds heal.

When I was thrust into the role of betrayed spouse, I longed for validation, and I dived into book after book, trying to figure out how to navigate this trauma. I gleaned a ton of wisdom from the books that I read, but the same thing bothered me each time: as I read these books, there was a sense of detachment that I couldn't shake. I assume it was because the authors were writing about a time long ago and had many years of building trust and moving on between them and their great betrayals. The authors spoke so matter-of-factly. I found it hard to reconcile their lack of emotion with the great intensity of mine. Because of this, I felt compelled to write a book that could describe the intensity of emotion one feels in such a situation with raw honesty. My mission is to be completely open and honest with you about the unimaginable loss and life-giving triumph I have experienced.

Anyone who knows me will tell you I am a big nerd. I'm not necessarily the pocket-protector and chess-club kind, but I have an insatiable need to analyze and understand. The hows and whys of my confusion will haunt me and drive me to study and learn until I am able to answer the questions in my mind. With that said, I am no psychologist. I am no expert on addiction, but I have personally walked the road you are on. I have the agony of personal experience and the camaraderie of my battle buddies. One of my all time favorite authors, Brené Brown, says, "One day you will tell your story of how you've overcome what you're going through now, and it will become part of someone else's survival guide." My hope is that my experience can in some way help you with yours.

You have embarked on a journey of discovery. As involuntary as it may be, I hope you will fight to reclaim your identity. I would not have survived this chapter of my life had I not had the power of God within me through the indwelling of His Holy Spirit. My story, while certainly about pain, betrayal, and uncertainty, is also about finding peace, joy, and freedom. It is about my God, who mended all the rips and tears of my heart. Now, those weak holes in my heart have been filled by His Spirit and are the strongest part of me. My prayer is that it will be the same for you. I pray that He will sustain you through the pain to take you to the Promised Land. This land of joy and thriving is waiting for you. It is a reality that is not dictated by your circumstances but by the overwhelming love of your Father in heaven.

I would be remiss if I did not add this note: It is normal to feel like your spouse is a monster because of the pain you feel regarding his betrayal. My hope for you is that you not only run *into* the pain that has been bestowed upon you but that you will pray and receive eyes to see your spouse as God sees him. He has a complicated heart full of his own pain that has driven him into this unhealthy place. While he is still responsible for his behavior and the consequences that spring from his bad life choices, remember that God loves him too. Remember that God can and will redeem him if he surrenders to the Lord's holy power. You cannot control your spouse, but you can control the bitterness in your own heart by laying your wounds at the feet of Jesus, thus choosing your own healing. Whether you choose to stay in your marriage or you feel it is necessary for your marriage to end, I pray that you will still hold on to love for your great betrayer and, in the deepest part of your soul, long for his healing and complete restoration.

My Prayer for You

Sweet Father, my heart aches for the woman who picked up this book searching for answers. There are likely so many unanswered questions running through her head. I pray, Jesus, for Your supernatural peace to wash over her and give her patience in healing and ears to hear Your Holy Spirit's guidance in each and every step. Show her, Lord, that You are with her. May Your Holy Spirit intercede for her as You promise in scripture when she feels too overwhelmed and doesn't know what to pray. Help her to reflect on her primary needs right now whether it be safety, comfort, or maybe something that she can't even put into words. Help her to discover healthy ways to meet her needs with or without her spouse. Remind her of Your trustworthiness so that she may rest in the safe haven under Your wing and so that Your name will be glorified when she rises out of this pain full of joy, mercy, and confidence. Amen.

My Story

IT WAS THE SPRING OF 2019 WHEN I FINALLY FINISHED MY Snow White puzzle. The morning light bounced throughout my backyard. The grass, still slightly dewy, stood taller than it should've but felt good on my bare feet. I walked into my shed, my life still boxed up from the move. The open shed door escorted a cool breeze through the room. Steam, fragrant with cinnamon, floated into the air from my tea. I smiled at the quiet moment. I couldn't remember the last time I had felt this peaceful and, dare I say, carefree. I looked at the jigsaw masterpiece and noticed only a handful of pieces that remained unattached and stacked on the table. It had taken me a long time to get this far, putting that Snow White puzzle and my life back together. Many nights, I worked for hours and only placed a couple of pieces. Other nights, I powered through, placing a couple of dozen. As I placed the last jagged edges into their matching borders, the fairy tale of old was restored. One piece at a time, over time, God restored my soul just like that puzzle.

Dating

I SAT ON A BLACK PLEATHER COUCH ACROSS FROM MY SWEET yet sometimes naive college friend Stephanie a few weeks into the new year of 2005. We snickered on the couch as we watched her friend Carl stir a pot of stewed meat in a red sauce that caused our eyes to water and tinged our nose hairs with its spicy aroma. Carl and Stephanie shared some classes together, and he had shown interest in her. She wanted to be friends with him but didn't reciprocate his romantic interest, so she brought me along to kill any sexy vibes that might have emerged had it just been the two of them. Carl didn't flinch when we both showed up at the door. He welcomed us both with a giant smile and continued to tend to his culinary creation. We sat for a couple hours on one of the small couches that were standard issue for our small Texas college's dorm rooms, just chatting about love, life, and American culture. Later, we migrated to Carl's bedroom. Stephanie and I sat on the bed, due to a lack of space and furniture, and Carl pulled out his computer chair and guitar. We sang a selection of hymns and praise songs limited by the constrained range of our voices and Carl's guitar talents. The night drew on, and eventually Carl's roommate, Stephen, came home and stood in his roommate's bedroom doorway. He stood there tall and muscular, though his muscles were swallowed by a shirt and pants that were both three sizes larger than needed. A silver chain around his neck and a do-rag on his head solidified his rapper style. He was impressed at how much an unassuming white girl knew about Tupac.

"You did what for your assignment?" Stephen asked in disbelief.

"I wrote about Tupac's crisis-management plan." Three sets of eyes narrowed in confusion, so I continued. "OK, so our assignment was to analyze a crisis-management strategy. If Tupac is still alive, then he has executed the greatest crisis-management plan ever!"

To put it in context, Tupac had just released another new rap album, even though he had died seven years earlier. There were conspiracy theories, though it seems ridiculous now, that he had faked his death and was still alive and recording.

"OK, OK, I see you," Stephen replied. He may very well have thought I was oblivious for buying into the conspiracy, but his astonishment that I not only listened to Tupac but knew so much about his history, his work, his prison sentence, his gang affiliation, and his beef with rival rapper Biggie Smalls seemed to override any judgment.

I was happy to buck the status quo. Little did I know then that Stephen would hold my hand to the sweet melodies of Etta James as we walked down the aisle three years later.

Stephen was strong and kind. He played college basketball and was popular throughout the campus. I was the kind of person who had a small yet intimate group of friends. He was the standard big man on campus. Stephen was known everywhere we went. People treated him like a celebrity. When he arrived at parties, there would no doubt be a flock of peers who would rush to his side, ensuring he was taken care of by equipping him with food, drink, and anything else he might request. When I would go out with him, my ego would wince at how much more attention he got than me. However, he seemed to be respected, and I admired that about him.

Later, after Stephen became my husband, he and I would laugh about how awkward he was in those first days. At first glance, he appeared to be a ladies' man, but he just kept falling into these embarrassing moments with me. I went to hang out with him and Carl at their apartment one night. As we sat on opposite ends of the couch, he asked me the classic *Dumb and Dumber* hypothetical question: does a guy like me have a chance with a girl like you? Growing up with brothers, I was familiar with the delicacy of the male ego, so I felt a little guilty about how quickly I said no. I wasn't saying no to him per se, but I hadn't till then been without a boyfriend since the eighth grade and was finally getting used to the idea of singleness after a long bout of loneliness. He played it cool, though, and instead of pressing, he backed off just enough. He would call me "just to talk." We would talk for two hours about anything and nothing, and then he would say, "OK, I guess I will see you around." It didn't take long before his "noninterest" started to interest me. We hung out as friends for about a month before we inevitably made our relationship official over a chicken sandwich at the local Chili's. That is when Stephen officially became my boyfriend.

I felt delicate and safe with Stephen. I often stood as tall or taller than the boys I dated, but he towered over me. For the first time, I felt like a cute, petite, feminine flower. It felt so good to feel small, even when I was wearing heels. His arms wrapped entirely around my body like a warm blanket, offering me a safe place.

He asked me a lot of questions about myself—my likes and dislikes, my history, my dreams for my future. With most people, I was usually the listener. I had grown up helping others with their problems but not feeling like I had anyone to turn to for mine, so I really valued his listening ear and his thoughtful gestures.

We dated for two and a half years until our college graduation. During that time, our major conflicts were over the church, my panic attacks, and his sex drive. He reasoned that his faith was a private relationship between him and God and didn't like to talk about it, whereas I wanted to pick his brain and debate over interpretations of scripture. I had not yet learned the term "anxiety," but I was definitely experiencing it. While I had always been a worrier, I would find myself in these seizure-like episodes, aka panic attacks. Stephen didn't know how to handle them.

I hung out with Stephen in his bedroom a lot. His apartment was more private than my dorm room. The first time we made out on his bed, my mind wandered to the R & B music playing in the background and the way his hand wrapped around the back of my neck. All I could think about was how many times he had been in this exact position with other girls. I struggled with that thought for a while, but he continually reassured me. Eventually my intuition was silenced.

Our discussions would get heated when he questioned why I wouldn't have sex with him. I wasn't trying to be a tease. I just had a limit to what I was willing to do. I loved kissing and cuddling and touching, but I had vowed long ago not to have sex before I was married. I knew it was old fashioned, but my faith (and my fear of getting pregnant) had made up my mind. I remember telling him that if I wasn't grown enough to get married, then I wasn't grown enough to have sex. He was much more experienced than me and had a hard time understanding my logic.

As we got more comfortable with each other, I started to make myself at home in his room. Stephen was still in the kitchen when my foot felt something under his bed. I bent down to look at what I had run into. I saw a bright-orange basketball-shoe box with the familiar white Nike swoosh. Compelled by my curiosity, I opened the box, expecting to see basketball shoes, but instead, I found a large row of pornographic DVDs. This bothered me. Maybe that should have been my first red flag, but even in a Christian college, it wasn't all that uncommon.

I confronted him. "It's your prerogative if you want to watch that stuff," I told him, "but I am not OK with it. If this is something you're into, I am probably not the person for you."

"Oh, I don't really even watch them anymore. That is why it was under the bed. I'll get rid of them."

I felt skeptical, but I wanted to believe Stephen so badly. By this time, I was already in love with him. Could I really blame him? I wasn't having sex with him. *As long as he stops, it is no big deal*, I thought. I chose to believe Stephen had made the decision to quit and that his porn use was in the past. To my delight, I never saw it again during the time we dated. I had no idea the degree to which he craved porn.

We grew closer and closer. We enjoyed the same things. We'd go out dancing together or stay in to watch TV or listen to music. I'd laugh until I cried at Stephen's goofy antics. He was decisive and familiar. I felt like I had known him for years. We thought so much alike. He carried himself with strength and confidence, but he also bought me flowers and touched me with such gentleness. I had never experienced this magic rarity of hard and soft. He was perfect for me.

As college graduation crept closer, the unknown terrified me. I would hint at marriage to Stephen, thinking that the unknown would be more palatable with a partner, but he wasn't ready. My anxiety heightened, and I suffered from frequent panic attacks. Numerous times I found myself in a seizure-like state, convulsing uncontrollably with panic and unable to speak. While I looked like I had myself together on the outside, I started to feel unhinged on the inside.

Stephen and I both walked across the stage to receive our diplomas in May. After graduation, we continued a long-distance relationship as I returned to work my seventh year at a church camp local to my hometown. I began an at-home recovery course for anxiety and depression, stopped eating sugar, and started exercising regularly to try to clear my head. I felt older than the other staff that year. I was working with high school and college kids, but I was out of school now. I kept to myself a lot that summer. Instead of hanging out with the staff, I would go sit in the back during the camp sermons. Each week, a different group of people filled the cabins with different schedules and different activities. It was uncanny, however, how many sermons focused on the biblical story of Abraham and Isaac that summer.

Abram was an old man and had no children. He was close with his nephew, Lot, but he still had no descendants to call his own. God promised Abram a son, even though he and his wife were way too old to be having children. The Lord also promised Abram descendants as numerous as the stars. He and his wife, Sarai, waited over two decades for this promised child, whose name would mean "laughter," since that was exactly what Abram and Sarai did when they first heard the Lord's promise. Several years later, God changed Abram's name to Abraham, and his wife's name changed to Sarah. She gave birth to their son, Isaac.

I can't imagine how Abraham must have felt years later as he walked the unwitting Isaac up the mountain to sacrifice him as the Lord had instructed. Abraham had waited all of his life for this special gift, the precious life of his son. His faith in God was so unwavering, though, that he knew that even if the Lord wanted him to sacrifice his son, God also had the power to bring him back to life.

Each time I heard this scripture, my heart stirred. I knew I needed to give up the person I loved the most. I broke up with Stephen that summer, telling him that I needed to deal with my anxiety alone for a season.

Stephen did not agree with my reasoning, but after some push back, he let me go. I continued to work out my faith that summer, wondering what my next step would be. A secondary theme of spiritual leadership weaved through a majority of the sermons and devotions from that summer. I knew that spiritual leadership was non-negotiable for me in choosing a husband. If I were to marry Stephen one day, he would need to make public his private faith.

I got the opportunity to attend a Christian leadership program in Colorado the following fall. During my time in that program, I learned a lot about marriage and family and how to look at life from a biblical worldview. Though Stephen and I were still broken up, we kept in touch.

One of my program instructors invited me to attend a women's Bible study with her. I sat on the couch listening to the stories of women who were struggling with young children or who needed advice on how to peel barcode stickers off of their newlywed china. I was the youngest woman there and had not yet entered their season of life. We spent time praying for each woman in the room individually. As the prayer circled around to me, a stranger put her hand on my shoulder and looked me in the eyes. She told me that she'd continued to hear the word "beloved" over and over as she was praying for me.

I blew it off. I mean, what was I supposed to do with that? Who says *beloved* anymore? Not too long after, I received a card from Stephen with the Bible verse Song of Solomon 6:3 written on the cover, "I am my beloved's, and my beloved is mine." Stephen had no knowledge of this woman's prayer, yet out of the blue, he'd chosen this card with this scripture. The Holy Spirit had my attention. I had vowed not to get back together with Stephen unless I intended to marry him. This card felt like divine confirmation that he would be the person I was going to marry.

In my excitement, I tried to be cute and send him a card asking if he would be my boyfriend again. He had already planned to come to see me for the weekend. I expected that he would get my card in the mail before his trip and that we would reunite with fairy-tale magic.

When I picked him up from the Denver airport, I was happy to see him. I waited for the romance but was met with platonic pleasantries instead. I realized that he had not gotten my card. We stopped at a Bennigan's on the way to my apartment. I told him of the stranger's prayer and said that I had been praying about whether or not we should get back together. His deep-brown eyes gleamed, and his cheeks blushed. At that moment, four months after the breakup, Stephen resumed his boyfriend status.

I assumed that after I finished my program, Stephen and I would begin dating again and see where our relationship would take us. I assumed we would get married eventually, but I was also painfully aware that just six months prior Stephen had had no intention of getting married anytime soon. We spent the weekend together, taking in the beauty of Colorado. He audited classes with me, and I showed him my new world. He fit right in, just like he had a thousand times before, perfectly adjusting to my life.

Stephen sat across from me to enjoy our last meal together before we parted ways for another eight weeks until my graduation from the leadership program. As we finished up our meal, he excused himself to use the restroom. He was gone for a lengthy amount of time, and I began checking my watch to make sure that we were going to make his return flight. When he finally returned, I just smiled, not wanting to embarrass him by inquiring into the length of his bathroom stay. He looked different. Uneasy, but happy? Nervous with a smile?

We each climbed into my '97 Camaro, buckled our seatbelts, and got ready for the ride to the airport. The ride was a quiet one, despite my efforts to make it light and fun. Stephen sat in deep thought, but I couldn't seem to break the barrier. *What is his deal?* I wondered. *Why is he being so weird?* The airport recommended that you arrive a full two hours early to get through check-in and security. We arrived around one hour before Stephen's scheduled take-off. I got out and unlatched the trunk of my car to help unload Stephen's luggage. He pulled my hand off of his bag and placed it around his shoulders. My other arm followed suit. His hug felt warm and safe, just as it had before. Butterflies fluttered through my body, and my cheeks flushed with romance. I savored the fleeting moment, knowing it would be at least two months before I would be able to see him again.

I stood on my tiptoes, raising to his lips to kiss him goodbye, and then lowered myself back down while keeping his gaze. Then his neck slipped through my arms as he knelt to the ground right there in the parking garage. He was on one knee. My heart pounded, and I felt dizzy with the intoxication of my love for him. I froze as I watched him open a tiny box with a ring. The ring was inscribed with the verse from the card, Song of Solomon 6:3, written in Hebrew. I barely let him finish his proposal before shouting "Yes!" through my involuntary grin.

We kissed, and then he ran. He was so late for his flight that he didn't have a second more to spare. He sprinted toward the terminal. I waited to make sure he got to his flight. He totally missed it. However, the staff was so touched by his proposal story that they rescheduled him for a flight out the next day free of charge. We drove back to my apartment, holding hands the entire way. I couldn't help but marvel at the fact that in three days' time, Stephen had arrived as an ex and was leaving as a fiancé.

Stephen and I spent the next six months in an excruciatingly tempting long-distance relationship. My love for him was intoxicating, and I couldn't wait to start our new life together. To distract myself from my own unsettled passion, I spent time with my mother planning our wedding. Stephen and I were married six months later in the Spring of 2008, on the three-year anniversary of our first date. Despite the surprise snow that inconvenienced us on that April date, the day was full of family, friends, and vows before God, with a playlist of serenades from Frank Sinatra, Nat King Cole, and Etta James. We stared into each other's twenty-three-year-old eyes as we said, "I do." We took pictures and smashed cake in each other's faces. All that was left now for Stephen and I was to live happily ever after ...

Questions for Reflection

⇨ Are there red flags that you ignored in your dating relationship?

⇨ If so, how have those flags evolved?

⇨ What healthy boundaries can you set around those flags today? For more information on boundaries, refer to the appendix.

My Prayer for You

Almighty Father, I pray for reflection and hindsight today. I pray that You will bring my friend clarity as she reflects on her early relationship with her spouse. We declare, Lord God, that You are a God of redemption, so I pray for patience and strength during this excruciating time of waiting. We know that You are capable of redeeming this love and this marriage if both parties are willing to reflect on their own shortcomings and do the work of healing and surrendering to Your Holy Spirit. May Your Holy Spirit guide during this time of reflection on the past as well as on the steps that must be taken toward the future. Amen.

Early Marriage

AIRY TALES AND STORIES FROM MY CHILDHOOD DEPICTED MEN who, after one glance, were so taken by particular women that they moved heaven and earth to be with them. These stories taught you to totally trust another person to rescue you, to take care of you, to love you. This conception of relationships in which you belonged to someone was central to my nature and to my conditioning as a young woman.

I was brought up to have the complex, dichotomous desire to both rescue and be rescued. Though I wanted someone to take care of me, I was also plagued by a hero complex that I couldn't shake. I felt like I could save anyone with enough love and understanding. I took pride in my ability to feel others' energy deeply. People felt drawn to that empathy, and I took their trust very seriously as they disclosed their fears and insecurities. I accepted my mission to fix their pain. I reasoned that I would certainly not be a good Christian if I did not do something to serve those who showed me their vulnerability. My purpose in life evolved into helping others. As a perk, I thrived on their compliments and praise. I found them to validate my worthiness as a person.

Without that validation, all that I had left was guilt and fear. Every decision I made was fueled by those emotions. Each mistake I made brought an onslaught of guilty feelings that beat me down. Once I felt terrible about myself, fear would pull up a chair and run my mind through all of the most horrific consequences I would suffer for my negligence. My impossibly high standards for myself overflowed onto those around me. I assumed everyone was driven by the same need to avoid those guilty feelings.

I craved that same validation from Stephen. Like all newlyweds, we came into the marriage with expectations—some reasonable, others not so reasonable. I expected Stephen to read my mind and fix my hang-ups and anxieties. Stephen expected a sex-fest and for my love to cure him of his insecurities. Neither of us got what we wanted. Sex with Stephen was not what I thought it would be. I remember the church telling me that sex was a gift in marriage. I wondered if I could return it. It felt uncomfortable at best and painful at worst. I have never had a poker face, and my lack of enthusiasm in the bedroom dulled whatever fantasy Stephen had conjured up during our years of dating. My anxiety had improved but was certainly not cured. When I felt panicked, I wanted Stephen to reassure me and calm my fears. He preferred to avoid the subject altogether or just tell me I should feel better. Both of us were wading in some newlywed disillusionment.

I firmly believed it was my wifely duty to help him and make life as easy as possible for him. I paid the bills. I cooked the meals. I cleaned our home. I identified as his "helpmate" and wanted to make my family and my God proud. I internalized the idea that the home is the woman's domain, so I rarely asked for help. I eventually got my own full-time job, so as time went on, I started to stew as I worked on the house and Stephen sat in his recliner. Still, I feared to rock the boat too much. If I asked for help, would he get mad? If I complained too much, would he go find someone better? Abandonment was the one circumstance that I could not see myself surviving.

Three weeks into my marriage, I found myself looking at the snow covering the ground outside our new apartment in Colorado. Stephen had already left for work and wouldn't be home for eight or nine more hours. I began to putter around the apartment, looking for ways to be productive. I continued unpacking and combining what few possessions we owned while I waited to hear back from any of the employers that I had sent my resume.

What is this? I asked myself as I sorted through Stephen's belongings, putting them away. I opened his college gym bag and found a stack of composition notebooks, like the ones you use to answer essay questions on a test. My writer's curiosity urged me to flip through their pages. As I scanned, I realized the contents were not academic but personal. I smiled. I thought only girls kept diaries. I slowed down and read more intently. I held my breath. Tears welled in my eyes as I read Stephen's innermost thoughts; he prided himself in his sexual encounters. I couldn't believe what I was reading. I glanced at the dates and exhaled relief as I realized the entries were dated before we met. I flipped over several pages to the dates we were together and, to my horror, read an account of him sleeping with his ex-girlfriend while I was away working for the summer. My vision blurred as I read through the tears. At the end of his account, he recorded a self-rebuke for his cheating. He called himself dumb for succumbing to his ex-girlfriend's seduction because of his feelings for me.

My heart ached with a dull pain. I tried to focus on how long ago the encounter happened, but I couldn't help but wonder if I ever would have married him had I known of his unfaithfulness. How could I reconcile this breach of trust with the undeniable confirmation that I got from the Lord to marry this man?

I cried. I panicked. I almost ran away to my parents' house, but we had intentionally moved out of state so that we could solidify our union and the beginning of our own family. I thought the distance would force us to work things out. So instead, I sought respite at a friend's house. She prayed with me while I curled up on her couch, tearing through the delicately thin pages of my Bible for some wisdom. Galatians 6:7–8 (NIV) jumped out at me: "Do not be deceived: God cannot be mocked. Whatever a man sows, he will reap in return. The one who sows to please his flesh, from the flesh will reap destruction; but the one who sows to please the Spirit, from the Spirit will reap eternal life."

When Stephen arrived home that night, I confronted him. I hated that he'd done this! I hated that he'd never told me! I hated that this was coming up *after* our wedding! But … it was such a long time ago. We had barely started dating a few weeks before the encounter. God was so clear about me marrying him. We'd just gotten married!

"I'm so sorry," Stephen said. "I feel awful about it."

"Why didn't you tell me?"

"I was afraid I was going to lose you. You said yourself that that was your dealbreaker."

I stared Stephen in the eyes, searching for something, searching for truth and intention. His eyes were deep and soft. I loved this man.

"The way I figure it," I replied, "God would not have told me to marry you if we weren't supposed to be together. Maybe He knew that I would have broken up with you if I would have found out before. I am choosing to forgive you, but I need you to assure me that it will never happen again."

"Of course. It was a long time ago. It never happened again, and it never will."

I believed what I had read in Galatians. God would not be made a fool of, and I was trusting that God would deal with Stephen in His own way. I also believed that God treated sexual sin with compassion. The more I thought about the situation, the more I rationalized it away. Stephen had not given his life to Christ when he'd cheated on me, and I had stood with him not three months before when he'd gotten baptized. He was a changed man now, I thought.

I depended on Stephen very much in our early marriage. For months, he was the only one with a job, so I depended on him financially. I also depended on him emotionally. I only knew two other people in the city, and they were busy with their own jobs and their own relationships much of the time. Stephen worked long hours. He left for work in the dark and came home in the dark. I counted down thirteen hours until his return. I had a primal need to belong. I belonged to him. I needed human interaction. I needed a deep connection. I wanted to feel his delight in me like I had when we were dating. I knew I only had an hour or two until he fell asleep, and I wanted to make the most of our time.

After he switched jobs and I got my own job, things smoothed out. We were truly friends and enjoyed each other's company. Our first year was filled with inside jokes and late-night trips to Applebee's. We were content watching fuzzy TV shows with an old school antenna before we could afford cable. We went to parks and tried out new restaurants. We saw movies and went dancing with friends. Our first year was full of laughter and love, passion and tears.

Several months into our marriage, I noticed a porn pop-up on our computer when I went to check my email. It was the first time I had seen porn surface in our relationship since the incident with his secret DVD collection in college. I felt mad and hurt and stormed the few feet over to him in our shoebox of an apartment.

"Why is there porn on our computer?" I raged.

"What are you talking about?"

"This!" I said as I turned the screen in his direction, showing a set of exposed D cups.

"I don't know what that is."

"What do you mean? You are the only other person that uses this computer?"

"I don't know what happened. It is probably from MySpace. I was on my page earlier, and it has all these pop-ups that come up on the website. I can't help what ads they put on their website. I wasn't looking at anything, but sometimes they come up randomly. I usually just close them out. I must have left my page open or something."

This was a different era in technology. Sure we had cell phones, but they were primarily used for calling. People were just beginning to text. Facebook was still a start-up, and I didn't know enough about technology to know if Stephen was telling me the truth or covering something up. I still felt skeptical.

So, I decided to exit the room with the last word, saying, "OK, well if you were looking at this stuff, fix it. You know how I feel about it." Little did I know that these isolated incidents were markers of a far bigger problem. Porn proved to be so commonplace, but I dismissed its importance.

While we may have gotten off to a rough start, marriage felt good as we put years under our belt. I liked the independence I felt from my parents. I felt like a real-life grown-up, and I was proud to be financially independent. We had moved to Colorado as idealists without any legitimate expectation of what it would take to survive in the real world, but there we were, making it happen. We followed job opportunities for Stephen that eventually brought us back to Texas.

We experienced ups and downs, but we were together through all of it. Sex got better and better each year, and so did my cooking. My career took longer to accelerate, but God continued to provide work each time we moved. I kept going to school and adding to my degree. Stephen kept getting promoted up the ranks. We were happy.

I would have told you that Jesus saved my life, but in reality, Stephen was my everything. Stephen was the person I looked to for comfort, wisdom, reassurance, and safety. I gave 100 percent of my trust to Stephen. I held nothing back. Sure, he had his issues. He struggled with anger, but I had trouble with worry and anxiety.

I never expected marriage to be easy, but I did expect to be cared for and cherished. I think that is why it hurt so much when I found myself seizing and screaming in the closet from panic while Stephen made himself a sandwich or played his video game, unaffected by my agony. Each time my needs would go ignored, it reinforced the idea that my needs didn't matter.

Of course, our marriage wasn't all bad. It was mostly good, actually. It was easy for me to rationalize away any hurtful behavior from Stephen. Usually, a little extra attention would go a long way in reconnecting us. The time I spent occupied with getting my master's degree Stephen would spend doing whatever he felt like doing. Other times, we would binge hours of our favorite shows on Netflix, cuddling and snacking. We could both go out together and coordinate our guys' and girls' nights out so that no one was left alone. It was a nice balance of freedom and togetherness.

Questions for Reflection

⇨ Do you tend to feel like you are obligated to help others or that you have to serve others to earn their love?

⇨ Reflect on your level of comfort with your spouse (sexually and emotionally). Do you feel the permission to be vulnerable with your spouse? Do you feel sexually inadequate or that you have something to prove in your relationship?

My Prayer for You

Abba Father, You have created us for intimacy. You exemplify intimacy within the Trinity and show us a seamless picture of interconnectedness. We long for an intimacy that is not just physical but emotional as well. Lord, we pray for our partners and what feels like their inability to be vulnerable and forthcoming with us. We pray for their minds and for You to allow their hearts to open toward You, the good and perfect One. Lord, we ask that You would help us to guard our hearts well as You command us to do without hardening our hearts. We pray against the spirit of bitterness and self-righteousness. We know that all have sinned and fallen short of Your glory. With that said, may we be strong enough to stand strong on our standards and not cave in to avoid conflict. Let us feel Your presence as we breathe You in deeply. Amen.

Five Years In

FTER A LITTLE LESS THAN FIVE YEARS OF MARRIAGE, Stephen and I had been through three cities, six moves, ten jobs between the two of us, one miscarriage, and the process of buying our first home. A few months before our fifth wedding anniversary, we decided to try to have another baby and start a family. Nine months later, we welcomed our first bouncing baby boy into the world.

Six months after that, I knew that going back to work was the right thing to do. I had previously worked as a human resources professional, but my job had often required ten-hour days in addition to the hour commute to and from work. I longed to stay at home to raise my baby. Motherhood turned my world upside down. Taking care of an infant is seriously hard. I survived breastfeeding, sleep training, sleep deprivation, a bladder prolapse, and postpartum depression. My firstborn was my little soldier, and we had finally found our rhythm. I dreamed of being a stay-at-home mom while my kids were preschoolers, but when I looked at our bank account, the numbers just weren't adding up.

Stephen and I were fast approaching our sixth wedding

anniversary. One year prior, our waitress had been surprised that we were celebrating our fifth wedding anniversary, saying, "You two look like you are still dating or newlyweds." We had been so happy until my third trimester and the newborn months wreaked havoc on our marriage. At that point, I was struggling with the learning curve of motherhood, and he was struggling with my lack of attention to him. Stephen had not been keen on the idea of me staying home. We'd been used to the financial luxury of having two incomes and no children. He had challenged me to "show him the numbers" to prove that we would be financially able to live on one salary. Maybe he'd thought I couldn't do it, but I did. I pinched every penny and outlined how we could make it on one salary. The last several months, however, we seemed to be a few hundred dollars short each month, and I couldn't figure out why. I assumed that I must have miscalculated in my sleep-deprived haze. I would come to find out four years later that that was not at all the case. Instead, the money I was short each month was paying for Stephen's compulsive sexual behavior.

Questions for Reflection

⇨ Are there big life changes that have seemed to rock your relationship?

⇨ How do you and your spouse deal with stress? Are your coping mechanisms healthy, or do you or your spouse lean into a destructive vice? For more information on healthy coping mechanisms, refer to the appendix.

My Prayer for You

Loving Father, we have all had roller-coaster ups and downs in our lives. Whether the events were positive ones, like moving to a new home or having a baby, or hardships, like losing a job or grieving the death of a loved one, the stress that comes with these life events can really rock relationships. When we don't know how to cope, we often find destructive ways to make us feel better temporarily. I pray, Lord God, that Your Holy Spirit would beckon to my friend. I pray that You would call her into Your safe arms. I pray she would find a refuge from the stress and find someone to confide in who can offer godly counsel. Remind my friend of her need for self-care and of Your invitation for her to surrender her stress to You. We love You. We trust that we will get through this and that You will be alongside us the entire way. Amen

Nine Years In

*F*AST FORWARD NINE YEARS. I HAD BEEN WORKING FOR ONE OF the largest school districts in Texas for two and a half years. In that time, we'd had another baby, and now we were sending both our babies to the same daycare. After a ton of financial discipline, I made the final payments on both Stephen's and my student loans. All of these years, I had blamed the student loans for me not being able to stay home with my children. I submitted my resignation, ready to be home with my three-year-old and nine-month-old. It took a few months to get the hang of our rhythms, but I was finally satisfied.

Questions for Reflection

⇨ What is a recent "win" that you can declare today? It can be as big as financial freedom or as small as remembering to move the load of laundry in the washer to the dryer. Take the time to celebrate that win today. Regardless of whether that win is big or small, find a way to let loose and do something nice for yourself in honor of that win.

My Prayer for You

Mighty Father, the world can seem so dark during these times, but we know that joy runs alongside sorrow. I pray that You would help my friend find joy each day. Help her to celebrate each win, big or small, and give her hope that her life is not over. Remind her that this is a season. The despair is temporary. She will thrive again. She will laugh and love and dream again. So bless her today by allowing her to find joy. Focus her eyes on the parts of her life that are good. May we give You the credit for those blessings and hold on to Your truth from Joel 2:25 NIV that says You will "repay the years the locusts have eaten." We declare, Lord, that You will not waste this pain. You will honor her devotion to You, and You will sustain her with glimpses of joy throughout her process. Amen.

Settling Down

AT THE PEAK OF OUR NEW RHYTHM, STEPHEN LOST HIS JOB. We scrambled through a stressful summer of selling our house, finding jobs, losing jobs, and being displaced. At the end of the summer, on August 31, we finally received the keys to our new home. The keys symbolized hope for normalcy and for starting a fresh, new chapter.

I remember walking through the trendy front door of our new house. We were greeted by charm and empty space, the house full of echoes and the potential for a playful life. I imagined this home filled with love and memories of baking cookies. I imagined it with tiny fingerprints on the windows, with the pitter patter of little footsteps and the sound of laughter. And ultimately, I imagined a happily ever after—a fairy tale.

Stephen and I marveled at the potential for our new life and whisked to the master bedroom to christen the house with magic lovemaking on the bare floor. My libido surged and my heart pounded with excitement. Stephen and I had been apart for almost a month, and I was ready to be embraced and loved by my hero.

Well ... the fantasy stopped there. The floor was hard. We

couldn't get comfortable, and not all of the necessary "equipment" was working. So after a time of trying to salvage the moment, we concluded that we were both just too exhausted and that we would have our time as soon as we got our mattress in the room. We had made it this long; what was a couple more days? We got dressed and drove to pick up our two precious little boys and my mom to come to share the dream. I was so excited for this chapter to begin ... until I read the first of its pages.

Discovering My
Husband's Secret Life

Trigger Warning: This chapter could cause you to relive your own experience of trauma. Give yourself grace and time to process this account. Take as many breaks as you need.

FEW NIGHTS AFTER WE MOVED IN TO OUR NEW HOME, MY husband turned to me in bed.

"I have something to tell you," he said. It sounded serious, but I am good at serious, so I turned to listen with undivided attention.

"I have been having discharge down there," he confided.

"Oh no," I said sympathetically. "What is going on?"

"I went to see the doctor a couple of days ago, but I haven't got the results yet," he said. "Whatever you do, don't Google it. You'll just see a lot of stuff on STDs."

Alarmed, I asked, "Is that a possibility?"

"No," he said quickly, "of course not."

I felt relieved for a moment until my curiosity got the better of me. I know there is much written about a human's fight-or-flight response, but I have found there is another option. It is called freezing. My curiosity compelled me to Google my husband's symptoms. Just as he had said, each website I scanned indicated he had an STD. I froze, closed my eyes really tightly, and hoped that when I opened them the information I was uncovering would have all gone away. At first, I felt embarrassment for Stephen in an empathetic way. I recalled my own struggles with a bladder prolapse after I birthed my first son years before. After my search, I felt embarrassed for myself. I imagined a bright neon light above my head saying that I wasn't enough to keep Stephen's attention. All I could do was hope I was missing something and that my fears were completely off base.

⸻

Several days after his late-night confessional, Stephen told me he was being treated for chlamydia. He told me something about the test results coming back with an odd reading. He said he tested positive on one part and negative on another part.

"How could that be?" I questioned.

"I don't know. I was confused too. I wonder if I got it from a public toilet seat," he replied.

Of course, that didn't sound right to me, but I was in denial. He assured me again and again that he had not cheated on me but told me that the doctor had recommended that I get checked out as well and that we could not have sex for two weeks.

I felt regrettably ignorant. I mean, the closest thing I'd had to sex education growing up was people at school, church, and home all telling us to keep our clothes on and just don't have sex. From the number of teen pregnancies in my high school, it was obvious that not everyone followed the rules, but I was scared not to. I waited until I was married to have sex for a whole gamut of reasons.

One of those reasons was that I didn't want to have to worry about or need to be educated on STDs. Boy, was I wrong.

Unfortunately, my doctor's first availability was a few weeks later on my birthday. All the while, Stephen was feeling better after his treatment. It seemed as if his confession had lifted the weight off his shoulders, and now he hadn't a care in the world. He was cured. I, on the other hand, entered a dark place. I reasoned that if his treatment for chlamydia had cured him, then he'd definitely had chlamydia.

I lost trust in everyone. The person I had trusted most in the world, just undermined my trust and belief in human decency. My mind was flooded with questions. Could my friends be capable of the same deception? Was I a terrible judge of character? I tried to keep my secret from everyone for a time. Practically none of my friends had experienced anything like this with their spouses, so I panicked at the thought of their judgment. However, this secret was burning my insides. I kept the betrayal a secret for the sake of my own embarrassment but rationalized it by telling myself that I should keep the secret to protect Stephen's reputation. Even though he'd deeply hurt me, I found myself wanting to protect him and to protect the image of our family. I feared Stephen would lose the respect of our friends, family, and fellow church members. I thought, *What if he gets better but the damage is done?* I feared people would never look at him or us the same.

The pressure quickly became unbearable. I needed to talk to someone. After our weekly Bible study, I grabbed two wine glasses and a bottle of wine. I summoned my friend to join me on the back porch and verbally vomited all of what had been going through my head the past few weeks. I will call this friend Leala.

I had known Leala for about five years at this point. We'd first met at a Bible-study group similar to the one we were in now. I instantly liked her. I was jealous of her natural beauty, but her authenticity was contagious. I wished I could pull off leaving the house without makeup the way she could. I also marveled at how she had this way of asking borderline offensive questions but with an authentic sincerity that would prevent any hard feelings. She had a way of speaking her mind without anyone getting angry. I chose to tell Leala because she had a track record of trustworthiness. She was a great listener and felt comfortable praying with me. Leala was the kind of friend who is present. She may not always know the right thing to say or what to do, but she will show up over and over. I knew I could count on her. When our second son had been born, she'd come over every week with dinner to hang out, give me some adult conversation, and watch my older son at bedtime so I could put the baby to sleep. I supposed it was possible that she would judge my situation, but I knew she was a safe bet. I decided to trust her. She didn't judge or panic but rather, as a nurse, walked me through the medical precautions that I needed to take in a very calm and clinical way. She just listened and encouraged me.

——————

The morning of my birthday, I sat in the waiting room of my OBs office. Once they called my name, I stepped into the back hallway and proceeded to go through the motions, knowing that I would have to muster up the courage to ask for an STD screening. I held my breath as I stepped on the scale and as the nurse Velcroed the blood pressure cuff around my arm.

"So what brings you in today?" the nurse asked routinely.

"I am due for my well-woman exam," I replied.

"Oh, OK," she replied.

I sat through the standard litany of questions regarding my last menstrual cycle and other general women's health inquiries. Lastly, the nurse sent me to the bathroom to complete a pregnancy screening and then escorted me into an empty exam room.

"How are you today?" my OB asked as she began to prepare the instruments to complete my pap smear.

"I'm OK," I replied with a grimace as she inserted the vaginal speculum. I took a deep breath and started to explain. "Well, my husband told me that he tested positive for chlamydia and that I should get tested. It's a little confusing because he said something about the results being odd, but I guess I need to get screened for that too today."

I can't begin to describe the embarrassment I felt asking for that chlamydia screening. The OB told me that she would go ahead and order a couple of tests. As she walked me back out to the reception area, she reassured me saying, "If anything comes up, we will let you know right away, but I'm sure everything will come out fine."

I tried to block the problem out of mind as I sat at the dinner table that evening watching my sweet, newly four-year-old son and my one-year-old sing me happy birthday. I forced a smile as I opened cards and presents. I couldn't even appreciate their sweetness because my mind was racing with fear. There was nothing I could do now but wait.

The next evening, Stephen was packing for a work trip to his hometown. Since his parents still lived there, we had agreed earlier that he would take the kids with him so they could spend some time with their grandparents. That way I could stay back and get some rest to recover from the exhaustion of moving. At five p.m., while Stephen was upstairs packing for his trip, I got a phone call that began my spiral into D-Day.

The nurse on the other end of the line told me that my lab results had come back and I had tested positive for gonorrhea.

Frozen.

Confused.

Angry.

As my mind raced, I caught just enough instruction from the

nurse—prescription, Walgreens, whole dose, shot tomorrow, nine a.m. I called Stephen on my cell phone from downstairs.

"I have gonorrhea," I said in a cold, seething voice.

Silence.

"I gotta go," I said and hung up the phone.

On the way home from the pharmacy, I seethed with anger and confusion. Why was this happening to me? This was not in my script. I didn't have sex before I was married to ensure this would never happen to me. Why did I have an STD?

When I got home, I stood at the kitchen counter and downed a shot of some of the most putrid liquid I had ever tasted. When Stephen walked into the kitchen, I glared deep into his eyes.

"I have gonorrhea," I sneered.

"You'd thought you might've had it, right?" he said flippantly as if he was surprised at my shock.

Infuriated ... deep breath.

I interrogated him about him cheating on me. He denied everything. He reassured me that he had not been with anyone but me. I felt so lost and out of control. I cried hysterically into my betrayer's arms for two hours until he and my sons packed up the car and left for his hometown. This was certainly not the rest that I had planned.

"All it takes to avoid unwanted pregnancy and STDs is abstinence," my mother would say. She tried her hardest to be open with us about sexuality, but since her family had always avoided the subject when she was growing up, talking about sex still felt awkward to her. Even so, my mother made it very clear that sex before marriage was not OK by her, so we never talked specifically about STDs. I reasoned that if I waited until marriage, I wouldn't get one. As a virgin bride, my ignorance about sexuality extended my phase of denial and kept me in the dark for a long time. I was never exposed to anyone with an STD or an addiction growing up. My family was as straitlaced as they come. I'd had minimal exposure to cheating, and I didn't understand trauma or PTSD. I had no idea there were biological reactions that people have to betrayal trauma. My ignorance worked against me, keeping me believing Stephen's deceptions. Though I knew in my gut that something wasn't right long before the eventual discovery, I didn't have the slightest idea of what to do with that intuition. So I buried it. I wanted to believe so desperately that there was another explanation.

I arrived back at the doctor's office the next morning. I sat, tortured, and looked at the other couples in the room waiting to see their babies' faces or hear their babies' heartbeats while I was waiting to see if Stephen was cheating on me.

"So what brings you in today?" the nurse asked.

"I got a call yesterday that I tested positive for gonorrhea," I replied.

The spark in her eyes dulled.

"Can I ask you a question?" I stammered.

"Yes," she said with a tinge of judgment.

My voice vibrated as I explained, "I have never been with anyone else in my life besides my husband. I mean, I have never had sex with anyone else. Is there any other way besides infidelity that he could have gotten an STD?"

Any perceived judgment in her eyes was replaced with compassion. "There is no other way, sweetie," she said as she reached for my hand. "Infidelity is the only way."

Tears quietly flooded my eyes. The nurse was sweet as she walked me into the exam room. I broke down as I unbuttoned my jeans and slowly pulled them down to expose my left buttock for her to administer a shot. As I left the clinic, passing back through the couples having babies and people in for routine checkups, I wondered what had just happened to my fairy tale?

As I drove out of the clinic's parking garage, I drove into a mess of emerging PTSD symptoms and onto the ramp of an emotional and irrational roller coaster. Leala met me in a Wendy's parking lot as I sobbed. My whole life seemed to come to a screeching halt.

These wounds were abrupt and confusing; I felt completely lost and incapacitated. She didn't know what to say. I suppose there is nothing that one could say in such a situation to make that moment any less traumatic, but I needed to feel safe with my friend.

On my drive home, I couldn't help but recall the story of Hosea in the Bible. God instructed Hosea to marry a prostitute by the name of Gomer. His marriage to Gomer was symbolic of Israel's relationship with God. While God was faithful, Israel continued to turn away from Him. They not only chose to affiliate with Egypt and Assyria instead of trusting God, but they also began to worship other gods. Gomer was not faithful to Hosea. She habitually cheated on him and caused him so much pain, but even so, God instructed him to take her back time and time again. He used Hosea to symbolize God's unconditional and redeeming love. I pleaded with God, asking Him to please refrain from giving me a task like Hosea's. I didn't want to be Hosea. I begged Him not to give me that pain.

I had previously made lunch plans with another dear friend of mine. She was wise and full of life experience, a great example of Jesus's power to transform a life through the desire to study His Word. I had met Reba at a work conference, and we'd bonded over being somewhat awkward introverts. We were both terrible at small talk, so we had dived right in to get to know about each other's lives. She'd felt instantly safe to me. I chose to open up to her because she had proven trustworthy and had already walked alongside me through some serious pregnancy scares with my second son. I also knew that she had been affected by addiction in her life, and I desperately needed a level of understanding. When she arrived at my house, I sat on the back porch, numb and in shock. She helped me inside, and I told her what had happened. She bravely pointed out to me that Stephen's act of indiscretion was likely not isolated and prepared me for the reality that evidence of more infidelity was likely to surface. She seemed so strong to me at that moment. Because she had experience with loved ones' addictions before, she was competent to guide me through my feelings and very practically break those feelings down into questions to ask my husband.

I called Stephen and confronted him. I asked him how I was supposed to reconcile his denial of infidelity with the information I'd received from the doctor. I had caught him.

"OK, so I went to a massage place. I didn't know it was that kind of place until she went down on me. I stopped it as soon as she put her mouth on me."

"Are you serious?" I argued with him. "There are a whole lot of steps between getting your back rubbed and a blow job!" I boiled as I realized that he thought I was so gullible as to believe that. "Why? Why were you even at a place like that?"

"I don't know. My back hurt," he said defensively.

"Who referred you to a place like that?" I demanded.

"No one," he said. "I found it on the internet."

I proceeded to drill him about the name of the place, where it was located, when he went, and all of the questions I could think of in my frazzled state. Stephen answered a couple of my questions and then told me that his work break was over and he had to go. I hung up the phone.

I wept. Reba put her hand on my shoulder and gave me permission to lose control. My panic exploded into a big attack of uncontrollable seizing, pulling out my hair, crying, screaming, hitting the table, and finally collapsing. I was lifeless, unable to speak or move as she sat with me. Once I recovered from the attack, I searched frantically for the massage place to see if my husband was telling the truth. When I found the website, it was littered with portraits of girls looking lustfully back through the computer screen. There may not have been nudity, but it was obvious what kind of place they were advertising. I called him back. I yelled and screamed that I hated him. I cried out that I was broken and that he'd done it to me.

I couldn't sleep. My mind raced with all kinds of images and questions. I needed professional help. At three a.m., I started scouring the internet for a Christian counselor who specialized in sex addiction. Many of the counselors I researched did not acknowledge sexually compulsive behavior as an addiction, however others validated its legitimacy. Regardless of the semantics, I knew the effects of his behavior on me were certainly real. I must have scrolled through fifty bios before I found the perfect therapist. Her bio caught my eye. As I read it, I noticed her focus on biblical counseling; her areas of specialty included sex addiction and betrayal. I contacted her immediately through her website and requested a consultation, and the minute I woke up, I checked and saw that she had already responded, telling me that she had an opening that afternoon.

I emailed the therapist back to accept the opening. As quickly as a sense of hope came over me, it vanished and was replaced by fear. My heart raced with panic. I felt trapped in a real-life escape room. What would Stephen do? All my trust in him had shattered, and I feared what he was capable of. I started transferring money and packing bags like I was running from a serial killer. My senses were in overdrive, and my fight-or-flight response kicked in. I needed to get out of there. If my kids had been with me, I would have left, but my need for my children kept me tied to my home until their return. Betrayal thrust me into a world where my husband was a stranger.

Later that afternoon, I entered the therapist's office. It looked just like the movies, complete with a big white couch and soothing noises playing in the background. So many questions raced through my mind. I bulldozed through the pleasantries, wanting to make the most of the $140 I was spending for the hour.

"I have a friend who is a therapist, and I know the first meeting is supposed to be intake and rapport building, but I am really just here because I need expert answers to my questions. I want to make sure I have time to go through all of them,"

The therapist smiled and responded, "I think we will have time for both. I will go through the intake quickly, and then we can get to your questions."

We went quickly through the intake, and I provided various personal details like birth order and how long Stephen and I had been married. When it was finally my turn, I asked her about sexual addiction. How long had she been working with these clients? What was the success rate of recovery? Of reconciliation? What was the probability of relapse? What would this journey look like?

The standard model of recovery at that time labeled the spouses of sexual addicts as co-addicts. The idea was that while the addict is addicted to sex, the spouse is addicted to the addict by way of codependency. Codependency can be a little vague, but it basically means that someone takes responsibility for things and for people that they are not rightfully responsible for—a fixer. While I came to learn that I did, in fact, show signs of codependency, I would have punched someone in the face if they had called me a co-addict. I was traumatized and needed to heal before I was ready to accept any responsibility for the part I played in the dynamic of my marriage. Thankfully, the therapist was familiar with the baggage included in the co-addict model, so she took a trauma model approach. Her approach mirrored the model that therapists used for other PTSD sufferers, like veterans or rape victims.

The therapist answered all of my questions. She had counseled many couples in which one spouse was a sex addict and exhibited compulsive behavior in the same way that my husband had. She told me that marriages were able to recover if both spouses were willing to put in the work, and she suggested a book and workbook for me to order. She made it clear to me that I had no responsibility for my husband's choice to cheat or for his addiction. She knew, however, of the complexities common to any relationship and urged me to continue individual therapy as well as couple's therapy in order for me to grow and heal.

She explained to me that unlike with substance abuse, abstinence was not the long-term goal for Stephen. Instead, Stephen would need to explore his unhealthy view of sex and reprogram his brain in order to engage in sex in a healthy way. The first step in reprogramming his mind would be to complete ninety days of abstinence. Having no sexual stimulation at all for ninety days would force his brain to break the habit of craving sex to cope with life's stressors.

The therapist gave me permission to feel what I was feeling and explained that my panic and feelings of trauma were normal. She cautioned me that the story my husband told me was likely false. She warned that addicts only admit to acts in which they have been caught red-handed. Typically, she said, the addict will confess to what they cannot deny but nothing more. As hard as that was to hear, my gut knew it was true, and it was affirming to know that I wasn't overreacting. I knew I didn't have the whole story.

At the end of our session, the therapist gave me a homework assignment to work on. She asked me to create a divorce plan. I looked at her confused, wondering if she had been listening to me at all for the past hour. Why would she ask me to create a divorce plan when my entire reason for going to see her was to save my marriage, my investment? She had asked me to wait at least ninety days before making any final decision and had backed up her request by reasoning that my discovery was traumatic but so was divorce; putting one trauma on top of another would make things even harder to work through. Still, she urged me to figure out how I could leave and survive without my husband. If I chose to stay, she said it should be because I wanted to stay with my husband, not because I felt like I couldn't survive without him.

I left feeling better. For a moment, I felt safe, and the terror in my mind was on pause.

Stephen arrived home late that evening. I had spent the remainder of the day praying and journaling. I sat on the couch and waited for my husband to walk downstairs after putting the kids to bed. A supernatural, God-given peace came over me. I sat up straight, strong, and secure. I sat there in the awkward silence and looked my husband straight in the eye, waiting for an explanation.

I expected remorse, but instead, my husband opened with "Honestly, I did it because I don't feel loved anymore. I haven't for a long time."

I swallowed hard.

"How?" I argued as my mind recalled intentional acts of kindness, affirmative words, and loving gestures, like small gifts and love notes, that I had given him throughout our marriage. I thought of all the ways I'd tried to make life easier for him, of the times I'd saved him from his own anger by fixing his problems or the times I'd worked well into the night while he sat on the couch and got his rest. I couldn't believe that he would turn this around to make it my fault after I had affirmed him and sacrificed so much for him.

"I'm sorry you don't feel loved, but instead of telling me how you felt, you went out and cheated on me. That's on you. My hands are clean. There is nothing that *I* have done to justify what *you* have done." I paused. "I think it would be best if you slept in the guest room for now."

He gave a small nod and proceeded to walk up the stairs. On his way up, I gave him a handwritten note that I had written earlier in the day. As I'd written the note in the afternoon sunlight of our bathroom, I'd breathed slowly and deeply. I'd expressed to him that I was not sure if I wanted to stay but that in order for me to consider staying, he would have to agree to go to therapy and a weekly support group and to take therapeutic polygraphs as needed. We would also have to step down as leaders of our home Bible study.

Questions for Reflection

⇨ What are the top five things that you need from your husband to feel safe?

⇨ Note, you cannot be his accountability partner, but you can require him to get one in order for you to stay. This accountability community will be vital for his progress.

⇨ Also remember, this is his addiction, so he should take the initiative in making a plan for his recovery.

My Prayer for You

Holy Father, I just want to take a moment to breathe in Your Holy Spirit. As we breathe, may Your Spirit fill us. Fill the wounds and the emptiness with Your love. May Your breath calm our spirits and clear our minds for the moment. Lord, my friend is hurting and experiencing a pain that does not have an end date. I pray that she might be confident in Your presence. Be with her as she makes weighty decisions about her relationship and her family. May she be patient and follow Your timing as You provide her with clarity, step by step, showing her that this will not break her but instead, You will make her stronger.

Hope

Stand firm He says in divine whisper.
Following His voice, because I am lost.
Perhaps I am lost because I am just now listening.
Wasted time trudging through to make my own way
When there is only one way to freedom.

Tears fall as I am pierced by the thorns
Of this tangled mess I am in,
Of the thorn in my side.
While I bleed, He is gentle,
As He remembers the piercing pain of nails.

I am making my way back to you
In hopes that you will meet me
At the place of restoration,
The one place where hope resides.

I am making my way back to my future,
Hoping to see that you want to be a part of it,
Hoping that your scars will have new meaning,
Stories of victory and surrender.

Oh God, I hope ...
In the midst of despair, I hope ...
That when I get to restoration,
Our scars would come together
Like a locket; we wear our scars with pride,
Reminding us of the battle we won.

Oh God, I hope ...

Trying to Make It Work

AFTER DISCOVERING THE TRUTH, I FOUND MYSELF IN THIS hopeless place. I had quit my job six months prior, and I had two very small children. I felt trapped with a husband that I didn't trust. I didn't have the financial means to live on my own, even if we did split everything in half. I didn't even have the financial means to retain a lawyer. I didn't want to leave my kids without a father in the home. I wasn't emotionally stable enough to go search for a job at the time. I tried to protect my kids from the ups and downs of the emotional roller coaster, but honestly, my effort was largely unsuccessful. I would snap when my three-year-old didn't do what I asked the first time or when my one-year-old made a mess. I cried in a closet or in a corner while they played until they inevitably wondered where I was and came to look for me. I felt overwhelmed in every way.

Being the good student that I am, I started to work on my divorce homework assignment from the therapist. The exercise relieved me, but I still found it hard to wrap my head around the idea of my kids not having their father around all the time. The therapist challenged my thinking, saying that many couples who stay together for their children end up doing damage by modeling dysfunctional and unloving relationships for them. The therapist guided me to the realization that I always had a choice. She loved to see married couples reconcile after infidelity and addiction, but in her experience, she found that staying with one's partner for financial reasons and for the kids was not sustainable over time. The only reason for staying that had any chance of leading to long-term harmony was choosing to do so because I loved Stephen and believed that he could heal. So, I exercised my choice. I chose to give Stephen a chance at his own recovery. I chose to look at Stephen's actions and give his intentions the benefit of the doubt. I chose to commit to the process as long as Stephen was committed. I chose my own health, both physical and mental. I chose to let myself have needs, to express them, and to give myself permission to change my mind at any time. With each choice I made, the illusion of being trapped faded.

One of the most important choices that I made was who I let into my tribe. I knew I needed support, because I could barely breathe on my own, let alone take care of my house and my two precious yet very needy small children. Leala and Reba had proven themselves sincere. I knew that my parents couldn't walk this journey with me. They were too close, and I knew that their emotions would be too intense for me to handle. But I still needed someone who felt like family, so I called Wendie.

Wendie wasn't my sister by blood. We'd met by happenstance in college when we'd carpooled in the same vehicle to an out-of-town cross-country meet. As long as I could remember, people had been confiding in me about their problems, but most of the time I had felt neglected when I tried to open up about mine. Wendie and I connected in that way. We were both the kinds of people that others liked to use as sounding boards, but we couldn't always find sounding boards of our own. So naturally, we became each other's person. We listened to each other. We had so much in common, down to our family origins and the hometown politics we grew up in. She got me on a level that only a sister could. We had kept in touch over the past ten years, sometimes regularly, other times sporadically. Wendie was the kind of person that I could go a year without speaking to but then pick things up like no time had passed. We were both bridesmaids in each other's weddings, and we each acted as a constant safe person in the other's life. We had lived apart for several years after college, but now we found ourselves living in the same city. The tricky thing about Wendie was that we'd both met Stephen at the same time in college. She was friends with him too. Plus, she was pregnant. I felt selfish bestowing this level of stress upon her.

"Hey," Wendie answered the phone casually.

I sat on the other end in silence, trying to keep from sobbing. Her voice softened.

"Hey, what's going on?"

"I hesitate to tell you this, because I know you are friends with both of us, but I need you. I need my person."

"Of course, you can tell me," she replied. Later she told me that she'd thought at this moment that one of us was dying.

"Stephen cheated on me," I said, taking gasping breaths through the sobs.

"What?" she shouted in disbelief.

So I proceeded to catch her up and tell her what had been going on the past month. I needed someone who had been there from the beginning. Her shock comforted me in a strange way. I had been preoccupied, wondering how I could have missed the signs. She recalled the time that Stephen and I were apart while I was in school in Colorado. She'd seen Stephen regularly during that time. She told me how devoted he'd been even while we were broken up. She told me of the sweet things he would say to her and how she'd been so happy when we got engaged. Never in a million years could either of us have seen this coming.

In the following days, I devoured the book *My Sexually Addicted Spouse*. I pleaded with Stephen to tell me everything. I knew he was still holding back. He started by telling me that he'd naively visited a prostitute for a back massage that got out of hand. Over the next week, he admitted that he'd stayed until climax at the massage parlor instead of walking out. The story then evolved into him visiting various massage parlors twelve times over the past four years. Lastly, he confessed to having frequented the parlors sometimes as many as two to three times a week over the past four years. Each new piece of information stabbed me to the core, but this final piece took me out.

I ran. I literally grabbed my purse and headed out the door to my car. Leala met me at a nearby park. I thought I was dying. My heart was racing. I couldn't breathe. Before I knew it, my arms were twitching and seizing uncontrollably. I couldn't speak. Panic paralyzed me. Just one month ago, my fairy tale had to come to life with my dream house. I'd beamed with excitement at the prospect of getting to stay home with my children and spend the rest of my life with my strong, kind, and loyal husband by my side. Now I sat, exhausted from panic, feeling that my entire relationship—and life as I had known it for the last twelve years—had been a lie.

Leala drove me back to my house to get my kids. Even though she was already hosting her missionary brother-in-law and his wife, she welcomed the boys and me into her home and offered us the master bedroom for the night. She insisted that I update my parents. True to their natures, they felt a need to do *something* and started making the seven-hour drive to the city. I called Wendie. Without hesitation, she drove all the way across town late in the night. Leala, Wendie, and I sat at the kitchen table. I looked around the room in a hazy dreamlike state. Was this really happening? Surely, I would just wake up from the nightmare in the morning. To my horror, the morning sun only confirmed that this was my reality.

―――⟨⟩―――

My parents took the kids for a few weeks to let me have some time to process what I was going through and what I was going to do about it. Part of me wanted to run for the hills and never look back, but I kept thinking about the story of his proposal. I'd felt so sure he was the one I was supposed to marry. If God hates divorce, why would he have told me to marry this person just to leave him? Triggers came hard and fast. Anytime he didn't answer his phone, I panicked. I would call twenty times in a row and get more and more upset each time he didn't answer. He had an excuse each time, but I was really losing my mind. When I finally got a hold of him, he would chastise me and tell me that my expectations were unreasonable. Maybe they were.

The reality of the betrayal sank deeper into my soul. I felt like a worthless woman. Without my kids around to force me to get up, I didn't. I lay in bed, lifeless, without the motivation to eat or shower. I stared at the ceiling cursing my body, wishing that it would decompose faster. Saying that I was a shell of a person would be a generous description. I felt like a pile of ashes. Whatever fire, whatever light I housed within me had burned out.

Normally, I positioned myself as the giver instead of the receiver. I felt infinitely more comfortable that way, but now I had nothing to give. Leala had a key to my house, so she would frequently drop by to check on me. Once she and Reba caught me practically comatose on the couch and threatened to feed me like a toddler after seeing that I hadn't eaten in days. I had come to the end of myself, a place where my desperation was even more stubborn than my pride. The Lord provided friends who brought me food. A dear friend of mine was even so thoughtful as to bring me smoothie mixes and ready-made soups, since my trauma stole my desire to eat solid foods. All this time, I had lived in a gold mine of friends, but my need to look as if I had it together had stolen some of their sparkle.

Once I let my guard down, my friends showed up to bring food, watch my kids, sit and pray with me, or just hold my hand as I sobbed. My friends literally picked me up off the floor, tucked me into bed, and endlessly reminded me that I wasn't losing my mind. I thank God that my lack of strength allowed me to acquiesce to their help. For the first time in my life, I didn't care who saw me without makeup, even if they could detect last night's lamentations from the puffiness under my eyes. Each friend that I confided in supported me while letting me make my own decisions. They encouraged me to listen to God instead of getting revenge. They validated my feelings of anger but had enough self-control not to bash Stephen. I could see that they cared about Stephen too even in their anger toward him, and they offered to help by way of inviting him into their homes, providing accountability and the friendship of their husbands, and spending hours upon days in intense prayer for the both of us. In that season, I came to a place of vulnerability where I was unapologetically showing exactly where I was at that moment. While I didn't have enough energy for any other approach, the response to my realness paved the way for a liberation that stuck with me long after that season ended.

The therapist warned me that sex addicts experience withdrawals similar to those a drug addict would experience. She said that it happens on a lesser scale, but nonetheless, Stephen became increasingly irritable. One night when he was particularly irritable and it seemed nothing was going his way, I felt compelled to reach over and give him a hug. He hugged me tight and long. He told me he couldn't believe what he had been willing to give up for this addiction and that he was going to do everything he could to keep our family together. Oh, how I wanted to believe those words. I wanted to trust him. My vision grew hazy as I stared into the eyes of a person that I loved yet hated so deeply at the same time.

Meanwhile, the therapist continued to pull me back toward my own recovery. I would show up in her office wondering why Stephen was or wasn't doing this or that. I analyzed his behavior, trying to decode his intentions and verify his efforts. The therapist listened and validated but kept drifting back toward talking about the things I had control over and the steps I could take. After a while, I caught on to her pattern and began trying to intentionally focus on myself.

I discovered that I had very few boundaries, so I began the major task of creating protective boundaries around Stephen and his behavior. The concept of saying no felt foreign and wrong, but my overachieving, perfectionistic self tried hard to follow the formula I was given to develop some borders around the fragile ruins of my heart.

I sat down at the kitchen table and labored over labeling my needs. Primarily, I felt scared, overwhelmed, and incapable of taking care of others. So I started with those feelings. I felt scared; I needed to feel safe. I felt overwhelmed; I need time with God. I felt incapable of taking care of others; I need alone time to recuperate from my kids' need to be taken care of.

As I began to write out these boundaries, my heart yearned for Stephen to make me feel safe in the same way he had at the beginning of our relationship. I wanted him to be constantly reassuring. Terror flooded my mind as I thought about the possibility of him betraying me again. I couldn't take another blow. So my first attempt at establishing boundaries consisted of making rules to control my husband's behavior.

When Stephen returned home from work, I handed him a piece of paper that said the following:

My Needs: feeling safe, alone time, God time

Skipping Recovery
When you go to your recovery meetings, it makes me feel safe and feel that you are invested in recovery. If you were to choose to skip your recovery meeting to play basketball (or something

else), it would make me feel safer and give me space to process the trigger if you would find another place to stay for the night.

Cell Phone

When you take your cell phone into private places, like the bathroom or bedroom, without having a filtering program to monitor explicit sites, I feel worried and concerned that you have secretive access to pornographic materials that would hinder your recovery. Until you implement the Covenant Eyes program on all home technology, I would feel safer if you left your cell phone and computer out of all private places.

Check-ins and Feeling Texts

Check-ins and feeling texts help keep me informed about your recovery process and make me feel safe. When you do not initiate the texts or check-in meetings on time, I feel hurt and worried that recovery and reconciliation are not priorities for you. If you do not initiate the texts on time or check in on time, it would give me space to process that hurt if you did not come to family dinner.

Porn and Masturbation

Porn and masturbation are hurtful and devastating violations of my safety, but I recognize that you are early in your recovery and there is a possibility that you might slip. Because these slips would be incredibly traumatic for me, I ask that if you slip in these crucial ways, you leave the house for seven days. During those seven days, there will be no contact between us or between you and the kids.

Acting Out

Though I realize that you are a sex addict, I have an expectation that you will not act out with any other individual, including by going to massage places. If you act out sexually with any other person, we will indefinitely and possibly permanently separate.

Stephen responded agreeably but certainly not enthusiastically. He knew it wouldn't be a positive sign if he said no in the midst of my discovery of his betrayal, so he went along with my conditions. He resisted the separation from his cell phone the most. His phone seemed to be an extension of him, and asking him to leave its sight was like asking him to cut off his arm. He quickly negotiated for me to put a parental lock on his phone so it could accompany him to the bathroom. I reluctantly agreed.

While my first attempt at setting boundaries was a vast improvement over the complete lack of boundaries I'd had before, they still weren't ideal. Instead of trying to control my husband's actions, I should have taken accountability for mine. I came to a crossroads where I could blame Stephen for everything or I could start to own what I had tolerated. I'd spent years unaware of his secret vice, but I could no longer blame my ignorance for my pain. I stood shakily, like a wounded soldier surprised by gunfire but refusing to give up. I stood as firm as I could in the midst of confusion and self-doubt.

Setting boundaries planted seeds of self-respect to replace that which had gradually been choked out with each decision I'd made to sacrifice my own needs for the good of my family. My service had started out as a legitimate attempt to serve God and others. I'd justified my sacrifice biblically by quoting Philippians 2:3 (NLT), which says, "Don't be selfish; don't try to impress others. Be humble, thinking of others as better than yourselves." I'd made the mistake of believing that humility meant intentionally undervaluing oneself. But humility is not self-consciousness, self-doubt, or self-hatred. Humility is knowing exactly what you are worth and how valuable you are but recognizing that others have their own value and uniqueness as well. Humility is choosing not to compete in the pettiness of comparison but instead giving glory where it is due and celebrating others for their own unique gifts. My misguided attempt at living a good, Christian life had driven me to sacrifice my legitimate human need for self-care. My growth was stunted, and I shriveled as I ran around tending to everyone else's needs without tending to my own.

───────◆───────

I dumped one thousand puzzle pieces onto my kitchen table. The cover of the puzzle box showed Snow White sitting in the forest with all of her animal friends and a small cottage in the background. I had bought it at a consignment sale, hoping that Stephen and I could use the puzzle as a tool to be able to talk about his infidelity while having something to do with our hands.

I hoped that the intensity of our conversation would be lightened by the project and that Stephen's truth would come more freely if he didn't have to look me in the eye. In the same lane, I secretly hoped that I would be able to disguise my disgust as I kept my head down, given that I was unable to force myself to look at him most days.

I sat down across from Stephen with my own heart broken into pieces and started the daunting task by looking for the pieces that looked like Snow White. I knew I needed to put her together first. She was the center of this puzzle, and I knew the pieces around her would make more sense if she was whole.

Stephen and I had a couple of intense conversations at that table; I longed to decode the narrative Stephen was telling to try to justify his sexual encounters outside of our marriage. After that, the puzzle sat on the table for months. Sometimes I would sit and stare at the piles of pieces, alone and overwhelmed by the sheer number of them.

I finished brewing the coffee and set out an assortment of coffee mugs in anticipation of the arrival of our Bible study group. Stephen and I had led this Bible study for the past couple of years and had hosted it for the last five. The group had voted to study the book of James, a Christian guidebook of sorts that encourages Christians to act out their faith and exhort one another while compassionately praying and urging back Christians who have wandered away from the truth of Jesus. We greeted everyone with smiles and followed through the traditional catching up for the week while we got our children settled with the sitter. As the group members took their places around our L-shaped sofa, I looked at Stephen as if to say, "It's time."

Stephen addressed the group. He announced to everyone that he had not been faithful to me and that we were working toward reconciliation but that for the time being, we would be stepping down as the leaders of the group. He charged the group to decide who would step up and take over the leadership role. My instinct urged me to keep my head down and look at the floor, but I forced myself to look at their faces. I forced myself to sit up straight, with confidence, and choke down the tears that were so eager to fall at any moment. After Stephen spoke, I continued by saying, "We are telling you because you are our family here. James 5:16 says, 'Therefore confess your sins to one another and pray for one another, so that you may be healed. The intense prayer of the righteous is very powerful.' We need your prayers and your support."

The room was silent for what seemed like an eternity. The faces of men were stoic while the women gasped in shock, their eyes filled with pity. One of the men broke the silence and spoke on behalf of the group, telling us that they were all there to support us. Others in the group thanked us for sharing.

A fairly new friend of mine, though shy in groups, spoke up and encouraged us by sharing how she had seen the secrecy in these kinds of situations destroy relationships and telling us she was glad that we were bringing the struggle out in the open so that the group could help support us.

The small frame of my new friend could barely contain the size of her heart. I had met Ana in the nursing mother's room at church a few months before. I'd felt rushed yet thankful for a break to nurse my nine-month-old in the quiet room away from the hustle and bustle of Sunday morning. I'd felt a little intimidated as I had walked into the room and seen this trendy woman with pink hair and bright-red lipstick. *I could never pull that off,* I'd thought to myself, *but it is striking on her.* We'd struck up a conversation and found out that we each had two sons that were practically the same ages. She was a stay-at-home mom, and I had been desperate for some adult company after quitting my job. She'd invited me and the boys to go to the zoo with her the next week. We'd instantly connected via motherhood, God, and our journeys with anxiety. She'd instantly felt safe to me.

I had kept my trauma to myself on our playdates. After all, we had only been friends for a few months. I hated that she was new to our Bible Study and here we were dropping this bomb, but Ana didn't back away at all. She actually became one of my biggest encouragers. So I added her to my tribe.

My tribe continued to show up in my mess. One afternoon I lay crying on the stairs. My voice refused to sound. Leala called, and my toddler answered. She came right over and picked me up off of the stairs. She took the day off and watched my kids while I hid from the world under my covers.

Reba continued to pick up the phone each time I called. She helped me to analyze my situation. She gave wise advice and helped me understand what I was going through. She educated me on addiction and affirmed me. She stopped me from getting ahead of myself and helped me to focus on one day at a time.

Wendie consistently validated me. She allowed me to express whatever feeling I needed to express at the moment. I could be angry, hopeful, anxious, depressed. She reassured me that everything I was feeling was natural as she mourned with me with such authenticity. She mourned her own betrayal by Stephen, who she had considered a friend. We were so close that she felt the depth of my hurt in her own soul, and we grieved alongside each other as we tried to figure out where we had missed the signs.

Ana made herself available. She didn't shy away from hanging out with me because my life had suddenly become dramatic. We played with our kids together. She nurtured my children like her own and helped to distract me from my trauma. She gave me a break from my life. I didn't have to pretend around her, but she graciously followed my lead. She didn't force me to talk about my marriage when I didn't want to, but she listened when I did and helped me talk through my pervading thoughts.

The greatest thing about my tribe was their intentionality with me. They intentionally let me make my own decisions while empathizing with me and encouraging me to pray and seek the guidance of the Holy Spirit. Each one proved to be a true friend with her consistency over the long haul when I had nothing to give in return. I experienced genuine sistership that strengthened me and helped me to be brave, to reach out, and to follow through my journey of healing instead of crumbling underneath my heartbreak. I depended on their support, and my love for each of them grew deep roots.

It was mid-October before I saw Stephen's first breakthrough. After hosting our weekly Bible-study group one night, we sat back on the couch once the crowd had left and just talked. The conversation was pure, without arguing, begging, yelling, or stonewalling. He handed me a letter he had titled "The Fall":

> I'll never know how much I hurt her. I can't experience her pain and what I've put her through. I feel sick to my stomach and disgusted at what I have done. I can't express these feelings how I want to. A part of me wishes that we could go back to that fairy-tale life of obliviousness; the most difficult problems we had then seem so trivial now. A part of me wishes that I had stopped before this was out of control. It's far too late for that now. Of course, all of me wishes that I had never done any of this. If only I could go back. I would tell that hurt and exposed kid that this isn't everything. This is not what you have to become. This is not what you have to depend on. There is so much more in store for you. I would tell that little boy with the big brown eyes not to give in to the rage. Not to give in so easily to the asinine pleasures this world has to offer. I would tell him about the great life he was promised. I would advise him of the soul-leaching disease that would try to steal that promise and the destruction that would follow, tell him that he would eventually lose everything because of it. It's not worth it! It's not worth the pain you inflict on yourself. It's not worth the irrevocable pain you will inflict on those you say you love. How wretched could you be? How could you give up your kingdom for the lies of a thief? It seemed so blissful in the moment, so right being there … Then there's the utter misery at the moment your feet hit the ground again. You promise to never fall again only to let the lies sway you again and

again. It's like a nibble of a crumb growing into a gluttony-filled feast. I'm aware of you now. I know how you operate. I see your twisted mind for what it is. You feed on the insecure, the angry, the lonely, the prideful, the joyful, the content, the bored, the tempted, and the unprepared. I am forging my arsenal against your army. I will rise victorious against you with a hand of strength that is not of this world you fester in. Finally! But why did it have to come to this? Why now? The threat of losing everything is sobering, isn't it? I can't express these feelings how I want to, but I am a work in progress. I will be OK. But will they? Those who have fallen around us as this war wages on, are they OK? I just pray it is not too late. I pray that I may still be redeemed in their eyes. That I may be forgiven by all who have been hurt by us ... especially her ...

He wept in his shame and told me he was fighting for me. He acknowledged my struggle, and I finally felt like maybe he got it, even just a little bit. I let him hold me. It felt good to be wrapped up in his arms. It felt like home. He looked me in the eyes, something he hadn't done much since the discovery. He said he saw my pain and he saw my strength.

We went upstairs to watch a show. He sat on the couch in our bedroom. I invited him into the bed, and we lay together. I snuggled into his nook like I had done a million times, but this time I savored the feeling. I noticed his heartbeat. He broke down more, and I felt proud of him for releasing his emotion in a healthy way. For the first time, I felt the tiny whisper of hope that our marriage could survive.

That night started a phase of lust for me. For some reason beyond my comprehension, I craved my husband. His touch made me tingle in every place from head to toe. My heart raced and pounded like it had in anticipation of our first kiss. My body wanted him in every way imaginable. I just wanted to feel him closer. All the while, my mind argued and pleaded for me not to give in to lust. I had been pushing my husband to finish the therapeutic disclosure letter that was supposed to detail every infidelity. I had no guarantee that I had all of the information; it would be foolish to sleep with him after discovering his secret life. My rationale certainly didn't stop me from wanting him. I texted my tribe for backup. I couldn't resist him on my own, so I pleaded with them to reason with me and pray for my self-control.

By God's grace, I was scheduled for a road trip to my hometown to pick up our children the next day. That morning, I couldn't resist the pout of his lips. I kissed him—soft, slow, passionate. The flutter of butterflies felt so right and so wrong at the same time. My willpower barely held, but I was determined to stay on track with his treatment of abstinence for ninety days. Thankfully, I had somewhere else to be.

I arrived at my parents' house and greeted my kids with a smiling face. After their bedtime that night, I updated my parents on what had been happening. Disappointment framed their faces, and I could sense the hurt in their voices as they asked me questions about my plans moving forward. I defended Stephen to my parents and assured them that the God they had introduced me to was big enough to save my marriage. I could sense their restraint as they tried hard to let me make my own decisions.

I lay in bed that night exhausted and feeling so disconnected from Stephen. Just that morning I had yearned for him. I could barely keep myself off of him. But now, with just a little distance, he felt like a stranger again. That euphoric moment of connection fizzled with the miles, and my lust for him died out.

Once I returned home with the kids, I tried to force myself to be a good mom. I pretended to be present while my mind wandered throughout the day; I speculated about whether Stephen loved me enough to stop sleeping with prostitutes. Triggers still pounced fast and hard. Some would send me into panic attacks. While I vowed not to show my children the ugly side of my anxiety, I was rendered powerless under the spell of uncertainty.

I sat at my vanity gazing into the mirror. My mind downshifted into a state of merely existing when my baby cried and my toddler whined in an excruciating shrill voice that I could not tune out.

"Please stop," I whispered. "Please, I can't handle it. Stop. Stop! Just stop it!"

My kids finally paid attention as I fell from my stool onto the floor and started breathing in sharp, quick breaths.

"Just stop, just stop," I repeated, now speaking to myself. I didn't want to have a panic attack in front of my kids. I had to protect them from the damage, from my damage. Over and over I rocked back and forth as my arm began to convulse. I cried and screamed while my four-year-old put his tiny hand on my cheek and started to sing Anna Bartlett Warner's "Jesus Loves Me" to me in his soft small voice.

"Jesus loves me, this I know, for the Bible tells me so ..."

I loved him, and I hated myself at that moment. What a terrible responsibility it is for any child to feel as though they have to take care of their parents, but what a sweet little boy God had given me.

The trauma of my discovery still loomed over me as I sat in the uncertainty about the bounds of Stephen's infidelity. All of my capabilities would leave me while my mind drifted to the darkest of places. Was Stephen a monster? Had I married a sociopath? How far did his sexual deviancy go? Did he lust after children? Had he forced himself on other women? Was his infidelity merely transactional with prostitutes, or did he love another woman? Tears threatened to fall at any moment. If I dared to venture out, I could burst into tears if the grocery store checker simply asked me "How are you doing today?" I lost my keys, my purse, and my mind on a regular basis. I needed this pain to stop … and fast.

I sat on the therapist's white couch once again. This time Stephen joined me. He held his head down as he read from his disclosure letter. The list revealed time after time that he had cheated on me. He described in detail his first encounter at a massage parlor. He reported having seen an advertisement pop up while he watched his daily dose of porn. He confessed his curiosity about the massage parlors and said he had decided to give it a try. He'd paid for a massage and a hand job, but the prostitute hadn't stopped there. She'd climbed on top of him and proceeded to have sex with him. He described how distraught he had felt after that first interaction as he'd sat in the parking lot and cried in his car. The guilt had kept him away for a bit, but eventually he'd reverted back to his sexual compulsion. Once every few months increased to once a month. The more he'd gone, the more he'd craved it. Eventually he'd begun going once every two weeks and later, at his peak, two to three times a week. He confessed to having had sexual intercourse with at least five women and sexual contact with over fifty women. He denied picking up street prostitutes or pursuing sexual encounters at topless bars. He admitted that he had been to topless bars twice since we had been married. He confessed to viewing pornography frequently but denied any addiction to pornography.

I asked specifically about the nature of the pornography he

watched and whether he'd had any sexual encounters with children or underage girls. I suppose I felt some relief when he said that his preferred pornography was one man and one woman and that he'd had no sexual compulsions or attractions toward children.

I listened, but I couldn't feel my fingers. I felt numb from the inside out. I felt obligated to forgive him then and there. In hindsight, I think I felt like he would be so moved by my forgiveness that he would realize what a great woman I was and that that would cure any temptation he had for sexually compulsive behavior. It was not likely, but I could dream.

The polygraph following the reading of the disclosure letter confirmed that he had not purposely lied or withheld information in any of his disclosures, so I felt confident that he had written down everything he was able to remember. In a twisted way, I felt relief, as my imagination had conjured up stories much worse. At least I was sure of what I was dealing with.

I mostly confided in friends I had made within my church, but Sunday morning felt like a charade. A couple of months prior, Stephen had complied with my request that he confess his infidelity to our pastor. He'd used the word addiction in his explanation, but it was almost as if the word disguised the true depravity of his actions. The pastor almost immediately asked me if I'd forgiven him and if I wanted our marriage to work out, to which I replied, "No, I have not forgiven him. I just found out, and I don't know if I want to stay." The pastor basically responded by telling me that I would need to take those steps before we could move forward.

After Stephen's disclosure, I felt the full weight of his infidelity on my shoulders. I struggled with the images of him with the prostitutes that were circling my brain. I couldn't sleep for fear that the images would be waiting for me behind my eyelids. I found the lack of consistent outward manifestations of the addiction particularly disturbing. *At least you can see when a drug addict has been using,* I thought. I drowned in the constant fear that he had slipped up. How would I know if he visited a massage parlor or watched porn or masturbated?

So when the pastor approached me the next week, I openly confessed my struggles, hoping for words of wisdom or at least prayer. Instead, he responded similarly to before, blaming me for asking for too much information. I looked at him with disbelief and disgust as he continued to share how his sister writes a $10,000 child support check every month due to her famous husband's infidelity that resulted in pregnancy. Was he trying to tell me it could be worse? Did he really think that story was going to make me feel better?

I responded that I hoped our marriage would be saved but that for the time being I was just sticking around to see if Stephen would choose obedience or rebellion. That would be his choice to make, not mine.

I started to ask around about the experiences others had had with pastoral counseling at their churches. The reports of misguided advice bothered me. The mantra *God hates divorce* led misinformed pastors to urge women to stay in situations that were abusive and unhealthy. The reality was that my church and many others were filled with well-meaning leaders who were simply not prepared to deal with this level of betrayal. My experience confirmed that our situation required not only spiritual knowledge but the psychological knowledge of an experienced therapist who would be able to detect the signs of addict deception that often derailed unassuming lay counselors.

I sat down at the kitchen table, staring at the jigsaw puzzle pieces. The Snow White picture seemed to blur after a time, but as the details faded, I could see the colors. I just started sorting the colors—yellows in one corner of the table, pinks in the other. I separated the various colors of green.

As I sat there, I reflected on my tribe. They had proved invaluable, but none of them had had experience with sex addiction or infidelity, so I was still haunted by a sense of emptiness and isolation. Part of me wanted to tell everyone I knew, because I hated the secrecy and simply didn't have the energy to pretend everything was OK. But I didn't want to embarrass Stephen or ruin his reputation. I reasoned that this was the kind of thing that changed the way people look at you forever.

I began to refocus on the puzzle pieces, but instead of looking at the nine hundred pieces still out of place, I focused on one small pile at a time. I decided to keep Stephen's secret under wraps. I wanted to give him a chance to recover without dealing with all of the judgment. And with that decision, I placed two puzzle pieces together and rejoiced in the victory of getting one piece closer to putting my fairy tale back together.

—————

The therapist continued to reassure me that my symptoms indicated betrayal trauma and not a one-way ticket to a mental institution. Even so, I wavered between days where I felt strong and days where I wanted to collapse. I continued to learn healthy coping mechanisms and tried to put them into place. I still felt like an imposter setting limits with Stephen as I clumsily told my husband what I needed. I knew he could smell my insecurity, but I forced myself to shut myself up in my room to decompress when he got home, no matter how much I heard the kids whining.

I tried books, bubble baths, and meditation, but prayer served as my most frequently used coping mechanism. For most of my life, I had made the mistake of over-spiritualizing *everything*. Even so, prayer eluded me. Over the past several years, prayer had felt like leaving unanswered voicemails for God. This time was different.

My desperation forced me to give up control. I listened as much as I talked.

During that time, the voice of the Holy Spirit became conversational to me. I know that some, especially those who aren't intimately familiar with the Christian faith, will find that maddening or conclude that I was imagining the whole thing, but it was the most real and true connection I have ever experienced. The Holy Spirit's voice was kind and reassuring, not like my own thoughts, which were fearful or critical. Some days, I was too weary to even pray and I would just ask Him to speak to me ... and He did! Here is an example of what I heard from Him:

> Precious child, I am proud of you. I will give you
> the capacity to see as I see, but you must give up
> control. You must give up fear—not once, but daily.
> I will rescue you from the slavery of control. I will
> heal your body. I will heal your heart.

Prayer no longer felt empty but instead became my lifeline. I knew the Holy Spirit was speaking to me because the thoughts He placed would not have come from me. Mostly I would hear words as if the Holy Spirit was placing thoughts into my head. Sometimes I would see pictures, and other times I would get these intense gut feelings. The Holy Spirit stood by as a personal and gentle guide that helped to counsel and comfort me whenever I asked.

Later that month, we planned to attend a marriage intensive class given by the therapist's counseling center. My mother had arranged to come for a few days and watch our kids during the event. I could tell she was nervous when she walked through the door. This would be the first time she'd stood in the same room as Stephen after discovering his betrayal. I am the baby of my family and the only girl. There is a sense of delicacy that comes with that role, and the rest of the family feels they have a responsibility to protect. A part of my mom still saw me as a doe-eyed little girl with blonde pigtails playing with my Barbie playhouse. As a child, I would run to my mom when I scraped my knee. In my mind, she could fix anything. Only now, she didn't know where to put the Band-Aid.

As I opened the door, four little feet ran to greet her with shrieks of excitement. Stephen stood back, watching to see how she would respond to him. My mother set down her bags and hugged her grandkids. Immediately after, she walked straight over to Stephen. She looked him in the eyes and opened her arms wide. She wrapped her arms around him with the nurturing hug of a mother. After all, she considered him her son. Our eyes watered with relief.

Stephen whispered, "I am sorry. It will never happen again."

Mom and I sat on the couch in a moment of confidentiality. I spilled out my thoughts, as I often did with my mom, in an attempt to process my situation and make sense of it. As we talked, my mom was processing her own story. My mom had come to visit us several times, staying for a week or two at a time and helping with the kids when we were in a pinch. She began to recall events of the past.

"I remember having a creepy feeling one time when I stayed with you. Stephen was working from home. He reminded me all week that he goes out on Thursdays. He must have told me ten times. He said he would work at a restaurant to get out of the house."

She talked slowly. I watched as her eyes shifted, channeling her memory.

"On Thursday, I was in the loft folding laundry while you were at work. I heard the shower running for a long time. I heard him cutting his hair. He left the door to your bedroom open. He stood in front of the mirror in several different outfits. I wondered why he was dressing up just to go work at a restaurant. When he came out of the room, he smelled strongly of cologne and had a giddy smile on his face. He looked different. Creepy. It gave me a bad feeling. I wondered then if he was cheating."

The longer she talked, the angrier I got. Was she seriously telling me that she'd suspected Stephen's cheating years ago and never told me? How could she keep this information from me only to let me be blindsided into oblivion?

Enraged, I said, "You mean you knew … and you said nothing?"

"I wasn't sure. I didn't have any proof. It was just a feeling. What if I was wrong?"

I stood from the couch and escaped to the back porch. I felt betrayed by my mother. I paced back and forth across the deck. As I simmered, I realized that her story took place before I got pregnant with my second son. What if she had told me? What if I had left? My one-year-old wouldn't exist.

⸻

Stephen and I left early for the couple's therapy intensive. We arrived at the therapist's home, which was full of baked goods and snacks. My throat closed at the thought of taking a bite; I was too nervous. It felt awkward to know such a deep secret about the other strangers as they walked in. I didn't know their names, but I knew each husband was a sex addict. As the day pressed on, I felt relief to meet other women who knew exactly what I was going through. Most of us were at different stages of the journey. One woman had discovered her husband's secret life only two weeks prior. She was still a familiar hot mess of emotion. Another couple had been working on recovery for over a year and looked strong. A woman I'll call Chloe stood out to me. She'd discovered her husband had been soliciting prostitutes only two months before I found out about my husband.

As one of the exercises, our therapist asked Stephen and I to write a small, one-page paper that included a description of our journey and how we each felt after the disclosure and polygraph. Stephen and I sat in two separate chairs in the front of the room. He read his paper first, telling of abuse in his past and how he had gotten started with pornography. In his letter, he revealed new stories of infidelity that had happened during our dating years that I had never heard. My heart raced with panic. His voice faded into the background as I wondered again, like I had years ago, if I would have married this man had I known he was a cheater.

When it came to my turn, I summarized my discovery and told of the relief I felt after the polygraph. I concluded my paper like this:

> Ultimately, I have discovered that God is the only one who is strong enough to carry this burden. *He* is consistent. *He* is trustworthy. If I keep my eyes focused on Him, I can see this for what it really is—a man, weak and wounded, enslaved by sin. From what I read in scripture, I believe that God has a special disdain for sexual sin. That is why it is explicitly mentioned so many times in reference to evil and immorality and why there are so many scriptures explaining what marriage should be and warning against its defilement. But I also see that He is incredibly compassionate for those caught in this sin. The adulterous woman at the well should have been stoned and killed for her indiscretion, but Jesus stepped in, asking the one without sin to throw the first stone. Jesus reminded those men then and me now that none of us are without sin.
>
> It is only by God's incredible grace that I am able to forgive my husband. But make no mistake,

forgiveness is not trust. Because of His grace, however, I am willing to stick out the uncertainty of our future, for now, to see if our house—our marriage—can be rebuilt one brick at a time.

I believed that wholeheartedly, and I readied myself to do the work it took to save my marriage.

The marriage intensive was filled with therapeutic exercises and other couples telling the group what their journeys looked like. Chloe told of how she had followed a trail of destruction, researching the chat rooms her husband spent his time in, reading reviews he had given online for the prostitutes he frequented, and even driving to find the apartment building of one of his favorite women. She told of how she had called five different therapists who told her they were not equipped to help her before she was finally referred to this therapist. As she spoke, my spirit resonated with her. The feelings she described mirrored my own. I had finally found someone who understood. I had left my phone in the car, so I tore off a sliver of paper from my notebook and wrote my number down to give to her. She smiled brightly and handed me a slip of paper with her number. I secured the paper to my notebook with a paperclip. I knew I would need that number in the future.

The therapist and her team sat at the front of the room and gave us a warning.

"Ladies, you are about to be triggered. Husbands, I want you to look at your wives faces as they listen to this song. I want you to see the emotion below the anger."

Little Big Town's song "Girl Crush" began to play over the speakers.

I breathed slowly, deeply, begging the tears not to come. *I don't want to be that girl,* I thought. *That girl is a lie. The prostitute, the experience, is a lie.* Still, I have never been able to listen to that song again.

The intensive event served as an incredible tool to inform us about addiction, to allow us to tell our stories among safe people, and to provide resources to use with our spouses as we all returned to our daily lives. I left feeling hopeful that our marriage could survive.

In the weeks that followed, there was a day-to-day pressure to recover that hovered over me like a helicopter trying to land, loud and with a sense of immediacy. True to my nature, I assumed that if I followed all of the rules and overachieved on my therapy homework, I would reach a sense of normalcy faster. Though my world still felt shattered, I forced myself to reach out and broaden my community, but I treaded carefully as if to avoid another bomb of betrayal. My trust and faith in people had taken a severe blow, and I soaked in the shame and embarrassment of my incapacity to handle myself emotionally. If I were ever to let myself cry, I couldn't guarantee that it would ever stop. I felt like I had lived an eternity in a week's time, exhausted by the looks of pity and the well-meaning yet unsolicited advice. So many people misunderstood sexual addiction. On one end of the spectrum, enraged friends told me to leave the marriage immediately. On the other, well-meaning but misguided friends told me to forgive quickly and honor the covenant that I had made in front of God to my marriage. I filtered my tribe down to those who simply supported me without telling me what to do, those who were capable of patience as I searched for evidence of Stephen's intentions.

The hope I felt after the intensive died quickly, as Stephen seemed to neglect his homework from the event. He consistently made excuses about work being busy. I felt hurt that he was not prioritizing our relationship. I began spiraling again into a deep sadness that overtook my ability to perform simple tasks.

Thoughts of death kept invading my mind. I would imagine myself in a car accident or just not waking up from sleep. I couldn't imagine suicide, but the thought of my life ending provided me with momentary relief. The darkness grew and became unbearable. One evening, after a terrible day of distress, I braved communicating my sadness to Stephen. I wanted him to see my pain and stay behind to comfort me. I wanted him to choose me instead of the gym ... but he didn't. I sat in bed, listening to the hum of his car fade as he moved down the street. I had tried to be so strong for the last two months, but I couldn't hold on. I felt a heavy weight in my chest. I cried so hard that I couldn't breathe. My soul ached with the agony of grief. The pain was too much.

"I can't do this. I can't do this. I can't do this," I repeated while I rocked back and forth in the bed.

Still rocking, I picked up my phone and searched for the least painful way to die. I didn't want to exist. I couldn't bear to take any more pain and suffering. *The kids are in bed*, I thought. *Stephen would have time to clean up the mess before they awoke. They would be better off without a basket case of a mom anyhow.*

The first result that popped up in my search was the phone number for the suicide hotline. I wasn't calling that number. Instead, I felt inclined to call Wendie. I resolved that if she did not answer, I would go through with my suicide. I tested God in that moment, knowing that Wendie rarely answered her phone. Did He really find my life worth saving?

I listened to the receiver as the phone rang once ... twice ... three times. Just as I expected, Wendie's voicemail message began to play. I heard her voice. I wept, unable to speak. With my friend's gentle prodding, I began to describe my helplessness through the sobs. I asked her how Stephen could be so callous to my grief when he was the one who had caused it. I told her I didn't want to live anymore. I told her it hurt too much. I couldn't survive this. As I continued to cry out to my friend, Stephen texted me: "I feel like God is talking to me through this song." He attached a file of NF's Wake Up.

You only get one life
But every time you lookin' at yours you feel like all
you ever see are mistakes
And the problem and the reason you could never
move forward in life
Is because you were never awake

As the song screamed for him to wake up, I screamed too. What was wrong with him that he couldn't see my paralyzing pain? I wanted to scream in his face and tell him to wake up and get home. I replied to his text saying as much. Wendie refused to hang up the phone until he arrived home.

When Stephen arrived to see me in my hopelessness, his eyes softened and welled with tears of compassion. It seemed as if maybe this time he finally saw the depth of my pain. He held me and ran his fingers through my hair as I buried my face in his chest. We cried together and talked. He held me close and listened. I had hoped for this reaction many times since discovery. I felt connected to him for the first time in a long time.

We lay in the bed, mentally exhausted from the emotional rollercoaster of the night. I asked if he wanted to watch a movie. I wasn't ready for him to retreat to the guest bedroom. I didn't want the connection to end. We turned on the movie *War Room*. I had heard of the movie when it had come out, but neither of us knew the plot line. I picked it, knowing the odds of being triggered by a Christian movie were much lower than a random Netflix pick. When we realized that the film dealt with infidelity and how God saved the couple's marriage, we both sobbed. I turned my head to the window. There in the night sky, the light beamed from the moon, glowing both up and across in the shape of a cross. The light mesmerized me as it shone bright in the darkness. The moonlight cross signaled the beginning of healing and the hopeful possibility of our marriage being restored. I decided that night that I wanted to stay with my husband. I told him that I was committed to him as long as he was committed to a life of purity, dedication to God, and complete honesty and transparency.

───◈───

The next six weeks felt somewhat better. I still worked to learn how to manage my emotions in a healthy way. I still made tons of mistakes as I fumbled around trying to change my behavioral patterns. I found it difficult to suppress my tendency to push past my natural capacity and try harder, but my body had a way of revolting against my lack of self-care.

Triggers still came fast and strong. Once, I sat next to Stephen, trying to relax and watch a TV show. A scene in the crime show depicted this woman going to get her haircut after she had received some disturbing news about the death of her son and his killer. The hairdresser started kneading the woman's head slowly and methodically while telling her to relax in a soft voice and enjoy the head massage. The scene wasn't sexual at all, but the mere mention of a massage sent chills down my spine. I got up off the couch without explanation, grabbed my keys and phone, and left for a friend's house. Another time, I ragefully threw rocks at the family computer on which Stephen had watched countless hours of porn. While those tactics felt good for the moment, I soon realized that those ugly coping strategies were creating more problems than they were solving.

I willed myself to start reading and studying. I researched addiction, hoping that my understanding would help me cope. I stayed connected with close friends and talked through what I was feeling. I started to exercise regularly to release some of my pent-up anxiety. I played music loudly to drown out my thoughts and sang at the top of my lungs. Much of it was worship music, because I needed those messages, but I also had my rage music with angry women singing of how they were going to stick it to their man for cheating. I put together puzzles, and they calmed me with each small piece I placed into the bigger picture.

I approached a crossroads. Would I let this hurt destroy me, or would I fight for a wonderful life? I had already prayed for God to take the pain away. I had tried to sleep it off, hoping I would awake from my nightmare. This was happening whether I wanted this to be part of the script or not. So, I vowed that if I had to endure this awful trauma, I would become the healthiest person on the planet.

Book after book, and one therapy session after another, I began an intentional climb toward recovery. Initially, my motive was mostly to feel better as fast as possible. I wrote an outline for the therapist of all of the hang-ups I wanted cures for and worked to fast-track my recovery, hoping that if I absorbed all of the information, I could compress my period of grief. This was not going to destroy me.

My vagina, on the other hand, felt destroyed ... or at least depressed. I believed her to be damaged, unable to feel any pleasurable sensation ever again. Basically useless, she would never enjoy manhood or slide a baby through her quarters again—a depressed tunnel of brokenness that used to be lined with hope and pleasure and God-given life. I turned to my TV for comfort, trying to find a movie to distract myself from my loss. As I scanned my dashboard for relief, a screen popped up with a series of recommended movies based on my viewing history. The recommended videos featured sexual content that made me physically ill. One pornographic film after another taunted me and convinced me to lose hope in my marriage again. I spent the better part of the night crying and trying to figure out how to remove the recommendations, delete Stephen's watch history, and add parental controls to pick up the slack for Stephen's lack of control.

Another day, I happened to be on my computer paying some bills when I got a notification on my computer that Stephen was signing into Skype. My heart rate increased, and my right leg shook under the table like a jackhammer. I imagined he was in a chat room soliciting some virtual sexual favors. When I confronted him about the call, he defended himself and said that he had applied to another work-from-home job and was interviewing on Skype. I froze in terror while my mind flashed back to all of the time and flexibility his previous work-from-home job had given him to pursue his addiction. I remembered what my mom had told me about her suspicions about Stephen when she stayed with us while he had that last job. I imagined the overload of stress it would put on the kids and I to have to stay quiet while he was working. I felt appalled that he would apply for jobs so soon after he had started his current job and that he had kept his application process a secret. Stephen kept so much information from me; the trust gap grew between us.

Snow White just sat there, broken for a month straight without any new pieces added. I got so sick of looking at it that I packed it up into a large box, but I couldn't bear to break up the pieces that I had worked so hard to assemble. I gently laid each section one on top of the other and stacked paper plates full of color-sorted pieces. I carried the box to the garage and set it on the workbench to go untouched and unnoticed.

I sat in my therapist's office as she made it a point to say that God was the only one who deserves 100 percent of our trust. I realized more and more that my dependence was misplaced. In order to place my dependence completely on God, I had to detach from and remove my dependence on Stephen. My health was currently dependent on Stephen perfecting his recovery, doing everything he needed to do so that I could avoid triggers from his behavior. He had all the power over my well-being.

As I began to see that God was the only one who felt completely good and safe and strong enough to carry my brokenness, I started to focus on that perfection instead of my earthly and imperfect relationships. I felt determined to take my power back.

I still felt anxiety that told me I would not be OK if Stephen did not act in my best interest, but as my thinking shifted, I felt the power necessary to make informed decisions about my relationship and to be confident in my choices.

With all that said, I was still broken and just beginning the tall climb toward independence. I embodied codependency. The therapist and my tribe continued to urge me to take care of myself and helped me to focus on what I needed. Those small steps I took to refocus my attention on my own recovery were instrumental to my healing.

My world continued to be filled with the constant demands and constant noise that accompany young children. My thoughts were consistently interrupted so that I could open a juice box or change a diaper or play superheroes, but I began to exercise regularly and intentionally ate healthier. I poured myself into friendships to fulfill my need for human connection. I read and journaled. I took long baths and sang my heart out. I listened to Christian meditations that filled my mind with scripture and truths about God and His character. I practiced deep breathing. I began asking for help when I needed it. I began saying no when I didn't have the energy to give. I stopped cleaning my house and even started letting people come over when my home looked chaotic. I started taking care of myself; I started valuing myself.

Stephen came in from a meeting with a church mentor. I had met his mentor while serving at our church. He exuded such confidence in Jesus, as well as a fatherly affection. He was sweet enough to come and give me a hug at church one morning when I was sitting alone and crying during the sermon. I felt compelled to tell him the story, and he offered to talk with Stephen man to man.

After Stephen met with this mentor, he plowed into my bedroom and declared his fight for me. He spoke with such authority. *He is finally ready,* I thought. I was drawn to his strength and mesmerized by his resolve to work hard to save our marriage. I felt valued for the first time in weeks, like I was someone worth fighting for.

In the weeks following, Stephen seemed like a different man. He was selfless and attentive. He was grateful and not defensive. His communication was gentle, and he took care of me. I felt like he was coming around and that he was finally beginning to understand how I felt.

It had been six weeks since the intensive. My husband seemed to be trying hard to keep up with his steps and groups. The sting of my discovery faded slightly. I still had trouble eating, but there were days that I felt functional again.

We walked to a local park one Saturday with the boys. I sat back, watching my baby boy sit in Stephen's lap as they swung. My four-year-old was excited to show us all of his big-boy tricks like sliding down the swirly slide, climbing up Spiderman ropes, and flipping over small bars. Another mom and her child joined us, and we bantered about the joys and challenges of having small children. We watched the cute interactions between my four-year-old and her slightly older daughter as he challenged her to a race to show off his "Lightning McQueen speed." This moment of normalcy was euphoric. We played together as a family, and it felt hopeful.

Stephen and I had arranged a co-op with two dear couples we were friends with. Each couple picked one Saturday a month to babysit all of the kids while the other two couples got to go on a date night. It was a great solution to free up time and money to connect with our spouses. It was our turn to babysit the kids. I remember beaming with joy as we all danced in our living room to the *Trolls* movie soundtrack. The roar of laughter and giddy kiddy screams filled our house and gave voice to the joy that filled the air. I danced without reservation. I bounced and shook in silly ways. I tossed my hair back and forth and paused to watch the smiles on the kids' faces. Later that evening, Stephen and I bundled all five kids in their coats and walked them across the street to see the Christmas lights on one of the most festive streets in our neighborhood. Every single house was lit with magical sparkle and cheer. I stared at the beauty of the glow. I focused on the words of joy and peace displayed in the decorations. I longed to feel that again. I wished for more memories like this one. We made our way back home across the dark street in the crisp air. We lined the kids up for potty breaks and jammies, and then we all snuggled up on the couch to watch a movie. I felt warm in between the cuddles of three of our little friends and my babies. I glanced across the couch to see Stephen cuddled up too. I couldn't help but smile. This was the life I wanted. This was my version of a fairy tale. These were the moments I found myself believing that my family could stay together, that we could beat the damage of his betrayal.

It was a time of great duality. On one hand, I was hopeful. I saw Stephen completing twelve-step entries during the evenings. He reluctantly agreed to put GPS tracking on his phone so I would know where he was at all times. He was kind. He still struggled communicating, but it appeared he was trying to make it work. On the other hand, I still found myself in a pool of distrust that I seemed to be drowning in. I consumed book after book. I prayed six times a day just trying to make some sense out of my situation. I prepared a Christmas card to put under the tree for Stephen's gift asking him to move back into the bedroom with me. After I sealed the envelope, I found myself in such a state of panic that I never gave it to him. Just thinking about it made my body shake and my eyes flood with fearful tears. I longed for our marriage to be saved, but I was still terrified of the amount of pain Stephen was capable of inflicting on me.

During the day, my sweet baby boys just wanted to play with me, and all I could do was sit stoically on the couch in a dazed stare. Menial tasks took the greatest amount of concentration and energy to execute. My four-year-old and one-year-old ran around the house while I sat listless on a couch in our garage that we had converted into a playroom. The kids played right under my feet, but they seemed so far away. My older son blurred as he ran around the couch banging on the garage door and turning the garage lock. I told him to stop messing with the lock, but in my daze, I didn't check it. When Stephen came home from his twelve-step meeting that night, he pressed his garage door opener and busted the cables attached to the garage door. He was furious. His frustration and anger panicked me. I apologized over and over to the point that Stephen scolded me for apologizing. I desperately wanted control over my life, but all my attempts had failed.

I sat on the stairs and wept. I told Stephen that I just didn't want to live anymore. Stephen scolded me again for my dramatic response, but I truly felt like I had lost my grip on reality and my motivation to find it. I couldn't keep existing like this. How could I have thought my life was a fairy tale? Why hadn't I seen the signs? I was trying to be strong, but the exhaustion in my body forced me into a stupor. I couldn't handle the pressure or the uncertainty anymore.

———

My breaking point introduced herself to me as I hid in the closet, crying and depressed, one afternoon. I rocked back and forth repeatedly in a primal panic for comfort. My four-year-old and one-year-old roamed the house again by themselves. I cried so hard I couldn't breathe. My mom called. My four-year-old answered the phone.

"Hi, Grandma!" my four-year-old shouted.

"Hi, honey. Where is your mom?" my mom asked with concern.

"I don't know."

My mom's voice shook as she tried to stay calm. "Can you go find her for me?"

"Um, OK," he said.

My four-year-old dropped the phone on the living room couch and ran into each of the rooms downstairs playing hide and seek for me. He found me huddled in the closet with tears streaming down my face. He hugged me tightly.

"Don't be sad, Mama. Let's play. That will make you feel better."

I didn't respond.

"Jesus loves you," he sang as he cuddled up to me. "Dear God, help Mama feel better."

I loved my son so much in that moment. The purity of his heart changed the story of my tears into love for him and hatred for myself for exposing him to such chaos and pain. No child, let alone a four-year-old child, should have the burden of carrying his or her parent's emotions. I knew at that point that something had to change. A moment of clarity washed over my brain. I had hit my personal rock bottom, and I decided then and there I would do whatever it took to be the mom my kids deserved.

My family had frowned upon taking medication for as long as I could remember, especially medication that might alter one's mind. I feared that taking medication for mental health would confirm that I was incapable of trusting God like a "good Christian" should. I categorized my anxiety as a spiritual issue, believing that my anxious heart was caused by a lack of faith. That is what I had heard from the pulpit time and time again throughout my life. However, at that point, I was willing to try anything.

I met with Ana to run through my reservations.

"A woman with diabetes would not be shunned for taking insulin just because her body didn't produce enough to break down sugars and carbs. No one thinks that is a spiritual issue." she argued.

"I never really thought of it that way," I responded. "I feel like my brain is so constantly stressed that I am constantly panicked and in survival mode."

Ana continued to tell me about her own journey with mental health. She was passionate about removing the stigma attached to taking care of our minds. She was the first person I had ever talked to who understood the inner workings of my mind. Few people had seen my secret breakdowns. I was embarrassed by them, telling myself I was weak for having them, but she related. My mother tried her hardest to help me through my bad days, but I knew she didn't understand. As Ana shared her story, I found her choices to surrender to therapy and accept her anxiety as a medical issue an indication of strength and bravery.

"Don't you just love when people tell you to 'just choose happiness,'" she joked. "I just want to look at them and say, 'Wow! I have actually never thought of that. Thank you so much! I'm cured!'"

"Yes!" I said with a laugh, recalling the countless times I had been told those exact words. Of course, I knew that most comments were well-meaning, but Ana knew the guilt I felt over feeling depressed in the midst of all of the blessings in my life. Ana's testimony finally convinced me that my particular anxiety was truly a medical issue. Without medication, my mind wouldn't even be able to sort through my day-to-day tasks, let alone dig deep into my own personal issues as I walked alongside my husband with his.

Leala had previously accompanied me to my doctor to get some follow up STD screenings. While I'd been there, the doctor had prescribed me some anti anxiety medications. I had picked them up from the pharmacy, but they had been sitting in my cabinet, unopened. I went home and searched through the medicine cabinet for the medication that I had been prescribed during that visit. I chose one of the three that helped with depression and anxiety. The first day I took it, I felt numb. The prescribed dosage was small, but my sensitivity to medication showed in its effect. I welcomed the break from my emotions. The intensity of my emotions had reigned for such a long time, and it was nice to stop feeling for a moment. After a day or two, though, I felt less comfortable with the lack of feeling. Ana suggested that I take the medication at night so that it had some time to wear off before morning. Once I tried that, the medication worked fantastically. My mind felt more focused than it had in months, and the bewilderment's easing helped me gain some perspective on my situation.

Christmas came around, and Stephen and I passed out the gifts to the kids. I felt grateful that we were together as a family. I loved watching the faces of our children as they opened each gift. Nothing quite intoxicates like the delight and wonder of Christmastime on a child's face. We spent the morning assembling toys and hanging out in our jammies. My four-year-old spent half of the morning trying to convince me that Santa was real. In the middle of assembling a Little Tyke trampoline, I felt the dissociation coming on. I had become accustomed to these sorts of out-of-body experiences. Though I was physically present, it was as if my mind hovered over me to watch the scene of a family spending quality time together on Christmas. I was truly blessed to see the smiling faces of my children. It was a day to breathe. The profusion of happiness pushed the darkness away for the moment. I soaked up any scene that felt like the storybook life I wanted.

In the weeks following Christmas, I continued my new normal of emotional ups and downs. I vacillated between days when I wondered when the train would stop—when I would get a break from my anxiety or illness or heartache—and days when I felt hopeful that we were beginning to move into the next phase of recovery.

Stephen still appeared to be truly repentant and worked diligently to love sacrificially, prioritize recovery, and rebuild the trust between us. The days after Christmas surprised me with connection and special family fun. I imagined what Christmas would have been like without him and felt thankful that that was not our experience. The children looked up to him so much, and

I could see their need for his approval. He had been much more attentive with each of them over the last couple of months, and I could see my older son really blossoming from the intentional time that Stephen spent with him. What a year it had been. I felt beaten down by all of the changes but relieved knowing that the year was about to end. I felt lifted up at the idea that a fresh start waited for me just around the corner.

Our family celebrated New Year's Eve at Leala's house with her family and some mutual friends, including Ana and her family. The kids felt big, as they got to stay up past their bedtimes and all of our motherly food restrictions were lifted. They had their fill of snacks and desserts and ran around without a care in the world. Stephen and I sat together with Ana and her husband. That night, I noticed how Stephen and I sat together as a couple with the comfort of the companionship of another couple. I had taken this double-date scenario for granted, but on this night, I noticed every nuance. We joked about Ana and her husband starting their diets early and working hard to resist the temptations of yummy, indulgent treats. I would glance into the next room to see our kids running and laughing and screaming with delight.

As the clock dial circled toward midnight, we gathered outside. It was a happy time. I held my eldest son in my arms as we watched the sky illuminated with rainbow bursts; we marveled at their beauty together. I squeezed him tight while I watched the reflection of the fireworks in his eyes and watched his dimples dent with joy as he smiled. This moment symbolized a new beginning, a marker to start moving on from the agony of the past few months. I vowed to focus my attention on my husband's intentions. I could not be more ready for another chapter to begin.

Stephen had been working on his assignment from the therapist to observe ninety days of abstinence. For ninety days he was to have no sexual contact at all, from watching porn to masturbating to sexual intercourse and everything in between. Early in January, I stepped into the guest bedroom where he had been staying and found him changing the sheets on his bed. He declared to me that he had officially completed his ninety days of abstinence. I felt proud of him and also a little nervous that he would expect us to have sex soon. The magic of our holiday connection lingered, and I decided that his hard work should be rewarded by inviting him back into the master bedroom. I picked up a pillowcase and started to help, excited to tell him my good news.

"So, I have been thinking," I said with a smile. "If you pass the second polygraph, maybe you could move back into the bedroom with me." I grinned from ear to ear in anticipation of his reaction. I just knew he would flash me a big smile, jump across the bed to embrace me, and tell me that he wanted nothing more.

"I already did a polygraph," he barked.

A jolt of stunned disappointment vibrated through my body.

"That polygraph was just for the disclosure letter," I reminded him. "This one is just to make sure that you are on track and have been honest with me since then. The therapist told us from the beginning that that was the process."

"We don't have the money for a polygraph. They are too expensive," he grumbled. "Whatever ... I'll figure it out."

"Wow, OK," I said in meekness. "The way you are responding is making me think you have something to hide."

"I don't have anything to hide," he said. "I am doing what I need to do."

"OK," I said and placed a pillow on the bed. I walked away feeling deflated and withdrew to my room.

The following Tuesday, I showed up at my weekly women's Bible study to continue our study of Hebrews. I had been invited by one of my good friends in our church group to attend the study in the fall of the previous year. I enjoyed the dynamic of women from multiple generations and life circumstances coming together to worship Jesus and encourage each other. That morning we took turns reading verses from Hebrews 13. When the reading circled around to me, I shakily read Hebrews 13:4, "Marriage must be respected by all, and the marriage bed kept undefiled, because God will judge immoral people and adulterers."

As we discussed the verses as I group, I felt empowered to request prayer for my husband and our marriage in light of this verse. So many of the women comforted me and reassured me that they had experienced the situation that I alluded to. They assured me that his behavior was not about me, and a few invited me to chat after the study.

I drove down the street and parked at the neighbor's house, where the group's babysitter watched our children. A small group of ladies rallied around me in concern and commiserated with me as they recalled the hurt they'd felt upon discovering the betrayal of their own husbands.

"How did you find out?" one woman asked me.

"I went for a checkup and tested positive for an STD."

The faces of the women changed immediately from the familiar #metoo expression to one of pity.

"Oh ..." another woman finally spoke up. "So your husband actually had sex with someone else."

I stood there mortified. The excitement of finding comradery vanished and once again I felt isolated as the woman with the worst marriage in the room. The women began to apologize, saying they thought I had caught my husband watching porn. Oh, how I wish that is all I had caught from him.

Questions for Reflection

⇨ Do you feel shame surrounding your spouse's addiction?

⇨ If so, where do you think that shame comes from? It's not your addiction.

⇨ What do you feel like his addiction says about you?

⇨ Do you have at least two safe friends with whom you could share the details of what is happening with you and your marriage?

My Prayer for You

All-knowing Father, I know what it feels like to be crushed under the weight of secrecy. It is such a hard balance between protecting your husband's reputation and also getting the help you need to recover. I pray that my friend would find at least two strong, Christian sisters to be able to walk this journey with her. Whether they be established friends or part of a support group, may she find someone that she can be honest with without feeling judged. As always, continue to protect her day to day and give her the opportunity to rest and grieve and the strength to carry out her responsibilities.

Hard

Like the diamond on my wedding ring
That is hidden in a drawer,
Removed from my finger
Because its symbol has become meaningless.

Hidden

Like a child with his eyes shut tight
Out in the open for everyone to see,
Only truly hiding from himself.

Hard

Like the diamond on my wedding ring,
Your heart has turned to rock.
My tears cannot penetrate.
My screams won't knock your walls.
Down into the depths of darkness, you hide
In plain sight; you smile,
And I wonder why you are not broken
Until I remember,
Callous doesn't feel.

I Gotta Get Out
of Here

STEPHEN RELUCTANTLY SCHEDULED ANOTHER POLYGRAPH FOR the seventeenth. I prayed fervently day and night in dread of what the result would be. The polygraph was scheduled on Stephen's night to go to his twelve-step group, so to ease my nerves, the children and I went to hang out at a friend's house for dinner. I thought the distraction would be good for me. When Stephen called, I answered with a smile as I politely excused myself from the dining room for some privacy.

"Hi," I said timidly.

"I passed," he said.

I smiled for a moment, relieved.

"But something came up."

I froze.

"It's not a big deal," he said defensively, "but I masturbated once in November. I had completely forgotten about it, so when the facilitator asked if I was intentionally withholding information,

I answered no. The polygraph showed deception, so the facilitator had to ask me a few times. Then I remembered."

"So, were you looking at something when you masturbated?" I asked, wanting to know if he had been looking at porn.

"No, it wasn't like that. It was just pressure. That's it. I think I was in the shower," he said.

"But you would have at least had to fantasize, right? I mean, to get an erection?"

"I didn't fantasize. It wasn't anything. Just physical." His speech started to sound snappy and cold.

"How many times did he ask the question?" I asked.

"Three, I think," he said curtly.

I felt hurt that he had kept this information from me. I also felt relieved, rationalizing that at least my husband had not had sex with another person. I was skeptical when he said it was simply a physical release and that he had not watched porn or fantasized with the act, though. I also wondered how the polygraph would show deception if he'd truly forgotten. Stephen tried to act like it was not a big deal, but he could sense I was upset.

"So, what? Are you going to make me stay out of the house for the week?" he asked sarcastically. My mind flashed back to the boundaries I'd written down for him months ago, which required him to be out of the house for seven days without contact if he watched porn or masturbated. I felt so mixed up at the moment that if he had not mentioned the rule, I would have probably forgotten about it. Now that he had mentioned it, I felt like I needed to follow through with my boundaries so he would take me seriously.

"Yes, I think that is a good idea," I confirmed.

I planned to take the days apart to process my thoughts and revisit where we were as a couple upon his return. Stephen sounded disappointed but agreed. I was still upset, but I felt good about the conversation.

I finished up dinner with my friends and then loaded the kids into the car to travel back home. After tucking the kids in their beds, I lay down in my own and looked at the GPS tracker on my phone for reassurance to see that Stephen was attending his twelve-step group as usual. I followed the indicator and expanded the screen to read the street name. Stephen's marker pulsed at the same road on which the original massage parlor I had discovered was located. I panicked. I looked at the GPS again, hoping I had made a mistake. Stephen had turned his tracker off completely. I hyperventilated as I imagined Stephen hovering over a prostitute. I called Leala and asked her husband to reach out and check on my husband. Leala reported that Stephen's phone went straight to voicemail. He had completely turned off his phone, evading all accountability for his actions. I sobbed at the torment of imagining Stephen with another prostitute.

A couple of hours later, Stephen came to the house. He walked with boldness into my bedroom, where I lay prostrate in desperation. I looked up at him with red, puffy eyes. He wore a basketball jersey and was carrying a gym bag full of clothes and toiletries, prepared for his time away from the house.

He stood in front of the bed, looked me straight in the eyes, and said with authority, "I'm sorry I didn't tell you about the masturbation. I am ready to work. I am ready to do whatever I need to do to make us work."

I looked him in the eyes with a piercing stare, my eyes full of detached indignation.

"I have been here agonizing the past two hours because I had no idea what you were doing. Instead of stepping up and showing me during your days away that you are committed to recovery, you chose to violate another one of my boundaries by skipping your twelve-step group and going to basketball. You turned off your phone and shut out all accountability."

"I just didn't want to hear it," he replied. "I was already in trouble for masturbation. I figured I might as well go play basketball."

His words disturbed me. His actions showed that he was capable of shutting everyone out to do whatever he wanted.

After he left, I prayed. The Holy Spirit prodded me and encouraged me to distance myself from Stephen for a season. I had reluctantly obeyed the Holy Spirit's promptings through my journey thus far. This time would be no different. I did not want to leave my husband, but I couldn't shake the feeling that this would not be the end of Stephen's rebellion.

~~~~~

After our conversation, Stephen left to stay with Leala and her husband, according to our set boundaries. A few days later, I peeked at the GPS tracker, curious about what he was doing. The tracker indicated that he was in a part of town that I did not recognize. I looked up the address and researched the restaurant to find it was a local place not unlike Hooters. Seeing him there created such intense emotions that it gave me physical pain. When would he stop hurting me? I cried again.

On Friday evening of that week, I looked again at the GPS. I am not sure what I expected to see. I kept hoping he would prove my instincts wrong. This time the GPS showed him at Twin Peaks, another place designed for lustful looks. I couldn't take the triggers anymore. I didn't have time to recover between one trigger and the next. I figured that a recovering sex addict had as much business being at that restaurant as a recovering alcoholic had being in a liquor store. I couldn't sit by and just let him continue to hurt me. I needed a break from the pain.

Leala and Ana teamed up with their husbands to come over and help me. My friends helped me calm down while their husbands watched the children. I asked for some time alone to pray. As I prayed, I felt a spiritual inclination to write my husband a letter and start packing my bags to leave. In the letter, I apologized for all of the things that I had done to contribute to the dysfunction of our marriage. I struggled to apologize for enabling his addiction, but I did. I had no idea that he'd had this secret life, but my codependency had unintentionally allowed him to maintain his addiction.

I had standards for my behavior. They were impossibly high, perfectionistic standards, but nonetheless, I worked incessantly to be the best mom, wife, and employee on the planet. Most days, I struggled enough with those roles that it left no time for me. I dutifully sacrificed my role as a woman and a human being for the "good" of others, including Stephen. I served. I listened. I fixed. I sacrificed. I did not take inventory of what I needed. I did not rest. I did complain a lot in the hopes that someone would eventually come to *my* rescue. When I tried to express my needs, I communicated disappointment. I didn't know what I needed, but I knew I needed something. I knew that I carried this burden of responsibility and felt that I "had" to or else everything would fall apart. I overstepped, trying to run Stephen's recovery for fear he wouldn't recover without my help.

Stephen remained responsible for his decision to step out on me, but my own recovery had helped me recognize that I had my own unhealthy patterns that I needed to own up to. In the letter, I told him that I felt like he was punishing me for setting up boundaries to protect myself by continually violating them. I said that it seemed that when he felt angry or lonely or upset, he gave himself permission to hurt me, and that was not OK. I told him that I needed some space to focus on myself without the constant triggers of being near him. I planned to separate for what I hoped would be a temporary period of time by taking the boys and staying with my parents. I needed distance to see things clearly. Finally, I wrote that he no longer needed to stay away from the house and permitted him to come and spend as much time with the kids as he wanted before we left.

I sealed up the letter and asked the other husbands to deliver it. They met Stephen at Twin Peaks and talked with him for a while. Meanwhile, I began to pack my things and sort out anything that had sentimental value to me. The following morning, Ana picked up my boys as I prepared to meet my parents with a load of my things that I would be taking for my time away. Stephen showed up after they left, and we sat on the couch in our garage and talked. He didn't understand why I needed to go, but he wasn't mad. He gave me permission to do what I needed to do to feel better. He hugged me with disappointment in his eyes and left to go get the kids. When he left, Leala helped me load my luggage into her car. We drove four hours and met up with my parents in a Kohl's parking lot. I transferred my luggage into my dad's truck, and my mom got into the car with us. Over the next few days, my mom helped me to finish packing the rest of my things.

I felt unsure of how Stephen would respond during this separation. I sat the kids down and told them that we were going on vacation.

My four-year-old asked, "What is a vacation, Mama?"

I bent down to his level and forced a smile. "A vacation is where you go somewhere fun for a long time. We are going on a vacation to Grandma and Grandpa's house."

We sat in the driveway on January 17, four months after my discovery, my mom in the passenger's seat and my four-year-old and one-year-old in the back with no idea that this was not an ordinary vacation. I looked at my dream house in front of me, took a deep breath, and drove away.

Questions for Reflection

⇨ Take time to reevaluate what you need. At this point in my journey, I needed space. I needed physical distance to help sort out my hurt, my rage, and my confusion. I know not everyone will be able to pick up and leave in the same way, but think about where you or he could go temporarily if you needed space.

⇨ It is a good practice to establish check-ins with your husband. Check-ins are recurring, private, uninterrupted appointments where you and your spouse can discuss progress in the recovery process. Have them scheduled for a certain day and time each week so that they cannot be avoided. What time and day would work best for you?

⇨ What routine questions would you like answered during your check-ins? Accountability questions? Questions about recovery progress? For more information, refer to the appendix.

My Prayer for You

Gracious Father, I pray that all of the outside noise would be dull enough for my friend to hear Your voice. There will be those who give bad advice with good intentions during this time. Help her to keep her eyes focused on You, regardless of what others say. I pray that she follows Your advice, even if it goes against what others would think is best for her and her family.

Might As Well Be Dead

Make your bed
And lie in it.
Feel her body
So you can numb your pain
At my cost.

I have lost
My innocence,
My dignity,
And my respect for you.

You are lost
And cold.
I am surprised
Your heart still beats.

Then again, maybe you
Died a long time ago,
Because life with the inability to love
Might as well be death

Separated

*T*HERE IS ALWAYS A CHOICE. FOR EVERY CHOICE, THERE ARE consequences. I uprooted my boys, left my closest friends, left job opportunities in my field, and practically moved back in with my parents. My deepest hope was that the separation would be temporary. I envisioned my boys growing up with both their mother and their father in the same house. I longed to stay in the life I had built in the city for the past seven years, but in the innermost depths of my soul, I felt uncertain. I had no confidence, no evidence that I could return to the fairy tale I had always wanted, but I still hoped. My choice to move came with grief, loss, and difficulty. I felt incredibly thankful for the generosity of my parents while at the same time grieving the separation from my tribe, who had held me up for the past several months.

After a week of staying with my parents, I felt like giving up. Stephen seemed indifferent. He called a few times with nothing more to talk about than the weather. If he wasn't going to fight for our marriage, I wondered why he hadn't just filed for divorce.

A few days later, I went online to pay my credit card bill and found a two-hundred-dollar ATM withdrawal made on the same day we left the city. My heart plummeted in anguish. After my discovery, I had found around ten thousand dollars in ATM withdrawals that I had assumed were primarily used for prostitutes. I suppose there was no real way to prove that, but Stephen was the kind of person who paid for a pack of gum with his debit card, so I couldn't help but recognize the sign. I had later discovered that he went to ATMs to withdraw money for massage parlors that were cash only or for places that he didn't want to show up in the transaction history of our joint bank account. I sensed in my heart that he had returned to his addiction. I felt as if a thousand thumbs were pressing against the bruises in my soul as I winced and wailed with pain.

Later that week, I saw another hundred-dollar ATM withdrawal. I contracted with pain again. Stephen called less and less. I couldn't believe that this separation was so unmotivating for him. I wondered when the romantic-comedy grand gesture would come, but as far as I could tell, it wasn't going to.

I prayed every day multiple times a day just to get through. My marriage appeared to be hopeless, but God remained hopeful. When I prayed, the Lord reminded me that He never tired of my questions. His eyes didn't roll in annoyance if I brought Him the same problems from the same roller coaster over and over. He encouraged me to reflect on my dependence on Stephen and my mother and to redirect that dependence on Him. He gave me permission to rest in the chaos and the uncertainty, assuring me that He is always at work. So I sat there in the eye of the hurricane, weirdly peaceful as long as I stayed there, under His protection. I was beginning to see tiny glimmers of joy hidden amongst my sorrow.

A deeper level of isolation nudged at me as I sat alone in my parent's garage apartment, which stood separate from the main house. My parents had been living in this renovated studio apartment in their backyard for several years due to the ease of upkeep required compared to the main house, which had three thousand nook-and-cranny-filled square feet to dust and mop and maintain. The main house had turned into more of a museum by this point, with antiques housed throughout the house, including in its four bedrooms. My parents offered to move back into the main house with my boys for a season to give me an isolated and soundproof place to cry and work through my grief. I was grateful for the time, space, and quiet for my overloaded mind, but I was also lonely.

In my small country hometown, I didn't know where to turn for support. I dared not venture too far out from the house for fear of the questions I might get from other townspeople. I had lived away for over a decade at this point, so my presence was out of place in our predictable small town.

The therapist recommended that I join a support group for betrayed spouses that was facilitated by another therapist in her office. I Skyped into the group and immediately recognized the face of Chloe, the friend I had met at the intensive therapy workshop a couple months prior. My soul breathed in the fresh air every time I saw a head nod in agreement or heard another in the group murmur "Mm, yes." I found healing among other women with whom I could share my pain. They truly understood what I was feeling from their own experience.

Stephen's "drug of choice" was massage parlors. Other sex addicts prefer street prostitutes, teenage girls, chat rooms, voyeurism, or pornography. I was surprised to find a group of women dealing with betrayal trauma and walking along the same road I was—trying to reconcile a marriage where trust had been destroyed by the assault of this perverted compulsion.

The support group served as a nice supplement to my therapy. Each and every story was a powerful reminder that I was not alone. As I started to realize that there were more women than I had imagined dealing with betrayal trauma, I felt more courage to talk and share. I even started sharing pieces of my story outside of the group and found more people to add to this underground community of women who knew exactly what I was going through.

I talked about the ups and downs with these women. They helped me evaluate and organize the events that had happened to me. My perspective broadened, and I began to experience significant progress in my healing. My confidence bloomed, which motivated me to develop an action plan with the therapist that focused on my next steps.

The comfort of numbness still tempted me regularly. I droned in front of the TV for hours. Like a toddler playing chase with its parent or a baby covering its eyes in the middle of the floor while playing hide and seek, I tried silly tactics to try to outrun and hide from my pain, but it lurked and stared at me continually. It was unnatural for me to lean into my pain. I tried to face it. I tried to control my story, but I was beaten up. Some days I just didn't have the endurance to fight. With the support of my new battle buddies, I felt encouraged to allow myself those breaks, because I knew they would never let me quit my journey to recovery.

I sent email updates to a few friends throughout this time and asked them to pray specifically based on the current situation. In a response to one of my emails, one friend reported knowledge of another woman, named Darci, in our church who was going through the same thing. My friend had asked Darci for permission to give her phone number out to me and encouraged me to contact her. I couldn't believe someone so close to me could be going through the same thing. I'd probably sat next to her in church or said hi in the hallway and had no idea of the craziness she was going through. So, I took a chance and texted the number.

Darci texted back immediately. The texts grew longer and longer as we told our stories—so long that Darci gave up and gave me a call. We talked with an immediate sense of familiarity. I knew who she was from church, but the familiarity was deeper than that. We were living the same life in so many ways. Our perspectives complimented each other perfectly. Darci became the person I could dream with. We voiced our hopes for our lives and stirred up excitement for each other's dreams. We were safe to hate our husbands and to vent about and bash them for their shenanigans because we understood the complexity of emotions. Our hate so easily converted to love and compassion because it stemmed from our immense concern for their recovery and our desperate desire for our husbands to live in freedom.

We laughed so much together. We inappropriately joked about the amount of money we spent on therapy, comparing it to throwing dollars in a strip club. The laughter medicated the pain, but when the pain felt too heavy, we cried. We loved and prayed for our husbands through the pain they caused us long after anyone else could understand why we stayed.

I also met many bitter women along the way. Some had carried their betrayal around for decades, attempting to callous their hearts and their identities. I didn't want that for myself. I didn't want to let Stephen's betrayal have power over me for the rest of my life. So, as hard as it was to continue through the darkness, I just kept going. I only stuck with communities that listened without judgment and allowed me to make my own decisions about my steps moving forward. The dependability and trust I experienced in these communities restored my belief in human decency.

Valentine's Day approached. Stephen told me that he was beginning to realize what he had done to me. He said it was hard for him to talk to me about those things. I felt hopeful at his realization and disappointed at his inability to connect with me. I craved his vulnerability and honesty. After everything that had happened, I still believed that he would pull through. I knew he was broken, and I expected that he would need to return to the prostitutes in order to see his own brokenness and vow to be filled with Jesus. I was anxious to see what Stephen would do for Valentine's Day. When I received a beautiful bouquet of a dozen roses, I opened up the card in anticipation. Inside was a beautiful note about God's love and being a daughter of the King. I glanced at the bottom of the card; it was signed by the members of my women's Bible study. I was overjoyed at their thoughtfulness, though I was admittedly still hoping for Stephen to come through. In the next couple of days, I was flooded with encouraging messages and care packages from friends. I realized at that moment that I had spent my life trying to earn love from others by serving them. As I received their thoughtful gifts, I internalized the truth that I was loved, regardless of what I did or didn't do for them. It was liberating to sit in love without obligation. I did finally receive a gift from Stephen. He sent me half a dozen beautiful roses. I opened the card, anticipating his thoughtfulness. The card read, "Hope you and the boys are doing well."

I was livid at the lack of sentiment after I had poured my heart out to him with my poem. I wanted vulnerability from him, but I was starting to realize that he might be incapable of giving me what I desperately needed.

After Valentine's Day, my suspicions were confirmed. I received an email from my husband who confessed to having seen a prostitute. He said he'd known he would go back to the massage parlors if I left. He immediately followed that confession up by complaining about the distance and telling me all the reasons why the separation was not good for us. Then, to top it all off, he told me that I needed to come back but that things couldn't be the same when I returned. He reprimanded me for not pursuing him more and for trying to control him. Admittedly, I had tried to control him in order to control my hurt. It hadn't worked, but of course I'd tried. Regardless, I was offended by his audacity in using guilt and shame to turn around and blame his actions on me. It was honestly something I would likely not have noticed if I had not had the space to rest and work on my own healing. Stephen knew that I was motivated by guilt, and prior to my own recovery, I would have believed that I had caused his slip up through my attempts to control him and would likely have returned to him at that point.

The following morning, my dad came into my room to tell me that lunch was ready. I couldn't hold my emotions in anymore. I stood there crying in my daddy's arms, sobbing uncontrollably with the pain of more rejection. My dad held me. I needed to feel the embrace. I felt like a little girl again, crying to my daddy because I had scraped my knee. This time, it was because my heart was broken.

In the weeks that followed, I felt so lonely. I deeply appreciated my parents for everything that they had provided: a safe place to stay, space for me to heal, care for my children, food for us to eat, and so much more. Even so, the feeling of isolation swelled. I hated Stephen for driving me out of my home and away from my friends.

When Stephen came to visit, my parents couldn't even be around him. I didn't blame them. They were certainly processing their own hurt. The kids were excited to see their dad, and when he arrived, we focused entirely on them. After the kids were in bed, we had a chance to talk. Stephen began to open up.

"I just don't know how I got so far into this dark place," he said. "I feel like I need to figure out what is underneath the addiction."

More words that I had waited to hear for so long.

The following morning we went to my parents' church. It is a little country church located in one of the smallest towns in Texas. The congregation fluctuates between twelve and twenty-five members, many of whom had attended the church when I was a child. No one knew the details of why we were separated, but that Sunday, the members began to tell stories about those they were helping with other forms of addiction. To top it all off, a guest pastor began to preach about Ezekiel 33, where the prophet is charging the righteous to confront others about their sin and warning the wicked that they will die from their iniquities if they do not turn from them. Ezekiel 33:7–9 (NLT) says,

> Now, son of man, I am making you a watchman for the people of Israel. Therefore, listen to what I say and warn them for me. If I announce that some wicked people are sure to die and you fail to tell them to change their ways, then they will die in their sins, and I will hold you responsible for their deaths. But if you warn them to repent and they don't repent, they will die in their sins, but you will have saved yourself.

I just kept thinking about how much God must love Stephen. The Holy Spirit had been practically shouting words of encouragement and warnings at him all day. My love was tempered by frustration. We talked again that night after the kids were in bed. I sat straight across from him with confidence.

"I need the whole truth from you," I said firmly. "I can't take the lies. If you lie to me again, I will file for divorce."

"I went back to the massage parlor twice, not once as I said in the email," he confessed.

"I heard a woman's voice in the background when you called the boys the other day. Who was that?" I asked.

"I don't know what you're talking about," he said.

"OK, how about this: have you brought another woman into our house?" I clarified.

He reluctantly answered, "I picked up a woman at an icehouse when I was hanging out with some friends from work. She came home with me, but we did not sleep together."

There was no way for me to know if he was telling the truth unless he took another polygraph.

"You would be a fool to believe that this addiction couldn't kill you. This is not the worst it could get. Right now, you are a slave to this addiction, and I just want you to be free. But I cannot return to the city without honesty and fidelity from you," I told him.

He committed again to working harder to fight for me and for his recovery. He turned the GPS tracking on his phone back on so that I could track where he went. We watched a recovery video together, and I listened to him promise that he would do whatever he needed to do to save our marriage. I still desperately wanted to believe him.

Stephen returned home. In the days that followed, his effort fizzled with the distance. The first day, he talked to me about recovery. The next day, our conversation was just small talk. After that, he called late when I was already in bed. When the weekend came around, he didn't bother to call. When my triggers flared, I sat glued to his GPS tracker all night. I followed him as he went to a Wing Daddy's restaurant and then later traveled to a location that I was completely unfamiliar with. My heart palpitated as I imagined him with the woman he had picked up at the icehouse. It was past midnight, and he had not even called. I imagined he was with another woman.

I called in a rage. "What's wrong with you? Where are you?"

"I am just hanging out with friends," he said, defending himself.

"Who are you hanging out with?" I chided. "Are they the same friends that let you walk away with another woman after you supposedly told them that you were trying to reconcile with your wife?"

"What do you expect me to do? Just sit at home? I am not going to do that," he argued.

He had shunned all of our mutual friends in favor of new ones who were single and five to ten years younger. He remained defensive while I remained heartbroken.

I called Leala in a hopeless furor. She walked me through the most amazing prayer. First, she asked me to imagine I was sitting with Jesus. She then asked me a series of questions. As she asked, I closed my eyes, focused my mind on Jesus, and welcomed the Holy Spirit to speak to me. I imagined sitting on the floor next to an empty chair in the middle of a vacant room. Jesus appeared and sat in the chair, and I laid my head at His feet not unlike Martha's sister, Mary. I imagined Him gently but persistently speaking to me, asking me firmly to give up control. He urged me to give Him my trust and my pain by laying them at His feet. As I hesitantly laid my burdens down, He ran his fingers through my hair and gave me a glowing ball of light. This ball represented the abundant life He had for me in exchange for leaving my burdens with Him. As my friend ended the prayer, I sobbed. I felt lighter than I had felt in months.

The next day, nothing about my situation had changed, but everything about my perspective had changed. I genuinely smiled as I enjoyed playing with my boys. I felt overwhelming gratitude toward my parents and my family for all of their support.

Around this time, the house across the street from my parents came up for sale. The outside of the house was shack-like. The chipped paint sparsely covered the wooden boards on the exterior, revealing numerous bare sections of the house. When my parents asked if I wanted to go walk through it, I obliged merely for curiosity's sake.

My parents and I fell in line and shuffled through the front door. To my surprise, the inside had been renovated. The floors were hardwood. The kitchen cabinets were new and touched the top of the ceiling like I liked. The bathroom vanity had been replaced, and the one bedroom was a nice size. The previous owner had ripped out the second bathroom and was in the process of turning it into a walk-in closet. It was the only room of the house that wasn't finished. The house was small, but there was a nice-sized shed in the backyard that I saw as a great storage space or bonus hang-out space.

I struggled with the house. I still held out hope that my marriage would be restored, but the other part of me knew it would be nice to have my own space. My parents and I were making it work, but our roles were highly confused. My children were living in their house. I felt constantly torn between my parental rules and their house rules.

I could see the excitement in my mother's eyes as she began decorating the room in her mind. She marveled at the amount of storage space the small house possessed and looked into my dad's eyes as if to telepathically tell him that she wanted to buy it.

I saw her excitement as threatening. I felt as if she were pushing me away from Stephen, and I didn't like it. I think she just wanted to protect me. After we returned across the street, I saw my dad staring out the front door window of the house. I snuck beside him, wanting to ensure that our conversation stayed between the two of us.

"Dad, please don't buy that house just for me."

"Sweetheart, it's a good investment for us. It's a one-story house, and your mom and I are getting older. We may not always be able to walk up and down these stairs. We are not going to buy a house for you, but if we do buy, you are welcome to stay in it as long as you need."

I released tension as I breathed out deeply, relieved that there were multiple reasons the little house would benefit them. They were known for having collected property like stamps over the years, so I hoped that Stephen wouldn't see the house as a sign that I was done with our marriage.

I decided to travel back home to the city. I had an appointment there with my doctor to follow up on my previous STD testing, but I chose not to tell Stephen I was coming. I needed to know what was happening when I wasn't there. I decided to stay with Leala. When I arrived, I passed by the house, so I knew that Stephen's car was not in the drive. He still had the GPS app activated, so I could confirm that he wasn't home. I wanted to go to the house and snoop to see what I could find. My friend wisely expressed her concern about my idea and told me that I needed to pray first. As I prayed, I felt the Holy Spirit telling me that His guidance was all I truly needed but that if I thought I needed to see for myself, I could go. I couldn't resist. I had to see for myself. Leala wasn't going to let me go alone, so we traveled together to the house. You would have thought we were FBI agents the way we were looking through drawers and cabinets. The house was messy, but there was nothing noteworthy, until ...

I opened the nightstand drawer next to Stephen's side of the bed. There, staring back at me in all of its truth, was a box of condoms. My husband and I had never used condoms in our marriage, so I knew they were for someone else. My heart raced with adrenaline while I took a picture with my phone for evidence. Disappointed again. Heartbroken again. There began another night full of tears.

The next day, I called Stephen and told him I was in town. When I stopped by the house to visit, the condoms had been removed. I decided not to confront Stephen directly, because my experience thus far had shown that he would admit things only after he had been caught. I wanted to see if he would voluntarily confess this to me, so I kept my findings a secret.

Stephen and I had a long talk on the couch that night. He thanked me for my unconditional love. He cried. He didn't go out with friends. He went to his twelve-step meeting. When I talked to him, it was like talking with two people. I could almost see the battle in his mind on his face. He would be soft and open one minute, and the next he would become hard and stoic. I pleaded with him again to stop his compulsions. I told him that Jesus was the only one who could save him. When we prayed together, we sat on the floor in our kitchen holding hands with our eyes closed. I tried to walk him through the prayer Leala had facilitated with me. I could almost see the instant that he shut down. He expressed vulnerability as he meditated, sitting there with Jesus. Then, in a moment of silence, his face turned dark and callous. I realized at that moment that there was nothing more I could do. Jesus had asked me to give up control, but instead, I'd fallen back into the illusion that one more conversation—one more thing said in the right way—would motivate his healing, make him feel the depth of my pain, and make him run with intensity from his addiction. In reality, this was a battle within himself. It didn't matter that the depths of *my* soul longed for him to experience freedom. Stephen's fight was the only fight that mattered: *his* surrender, *his* commitment. I could not fight for our marriage alone, and I could not fight his addiction for him. I promised myself that the only way I would consider returning to the city to be with him would be if I saw evidence of transformation sustained over time.

As I entered the onramp to make the seven-hour drive home, I called my mom.

"Did you buy the house?"

"Yes, we did. It should be in our name in a few weeks."

"Good."

My empathy and my pain kept pushing me across a boundary. My emotions kept calling for me to save Stephen, no matter how many times he betrayed me. My motivation wavered between a desire to save him from himself, a desire to save the kids from growing up without a father in the home, and my own desire to preserve the picture of family that I had in my head. I felt like I could save anyone with enough love and understanding. My ability to feel others' energies deeply kept nudging me into unhealthy places. I was not doing Stephen any favors by pushing for his recovery. One day at a time, I reminded myself that my helping had become enabling and that I needed to let Stephen make his own decisions.

In the weeks that followed, I made changes. When I prayed, I felt like the Holy Spirit was telling me to stay back and stand firm as Stephen made his choices. God's provision was everywhere I placed my focus as I backed away from the idea of control. I waited to see what Stephen was going to do with his space. And speaking of space, both my parents and I were relieved at the prospect of having our own spaces. We could allow ourselves to settle back into the more typical roles of parent and grandparents.

Stephen did not significantly change his patterns. I fell into a web of bitterness. My efforts and my investment in our relationship were not reciprocated. Stephen traveled to my hometown in April for the weekend of our anniversary and our youngest son's second birthday. The Lord guided me to stop probing into my husband's actions and to trust the promise of the Lord's protection and provision. In light of that word, I set out that weekend to love him without expectation, just as I would love a stranger. I knew the weekend would be loaded with emotion. There is nothing like a wedding anniversary to remind you of the pain you've suffered from your spouse's sexual addiction.

The first night of his stay, we went to see *The Shack* at the theater. The movie's depiction of God's love for mankind and our relationship with Him broke through our walls. We both cried in our seats while we vicariously celebrated the healing of the main character in the movie. When we arrived back home, Stephen presented me with a few small gifts that I found to be sweet, and we had a good conversation. I looked into his eyes while memories flashed behind mine of our friendship before his secret life had come to light. I felt joy at the fact that we'd had that relationship and sadness knowing it would never truly be the same again.

The following day we celebrated our son with presents and a guitar-shaped birthday cake topped with two candles. It was hard for my parents to celebrate with us, but I appreciated the willpower they exhibited for the boys' sake. Both of our sons beamed with excitement to see their daddy, pulling him this way and that way to show him every toy they played with and every new trick they could perform. It was a nice break from the drama.

Once Stephen left again, loneliness weighed heavily on me. I tried to avoid it or deny it, but loneliness has a way of making you pay attention to it. Before I was married, the idea of being alone for the rest of my life used to send me into a panic. That fear drove me toward marriage. In my mind, marriage was primarily about security and secondarily about love.

Like most things in life, marriage was not what it seemed from the outside looking in. I stumbled through the intoxication of the idea of forever, but the reality of my isolation as I sat alone on my bed sobered me. I had hermitted when I'd first arrived in my hometown. I'd known I needed space from my husband to deal with my problems and to get some perspective, but I'd hidden from the ponderous questions of the other inhabitants of my small, gossipy hometown. When people see you out and about, they ask kindly, "What are you guys doing in town?" What was I supposed to say? "I found out my husband is a sex addict who has been consistently cheating on me through most of our marriage, and I am just in town to see if he loves me enough to change or if I will have to file for divorce? How are you? Some kind of weather we are having, right?" No thank you.

Just imagining the glazed stares I'd get if I were to answer this question made me gag, but I couldn't lie. I am a terrible liar. I knew that about myself. So it was just easier to avoid people. When I was forced to answer, I'd just say we were visiting. Then the summer came, and I would say we were in town for the summer. No amount of southern charm could convert my situation in a grocery-store, pass-by conversation.

Since my discovery, I had waited to see what Stephen would choose. I was still waiting. By this time my waiting had become much more passive and calculated. I rarely pushed anymore. I was tired of the disappointment, so I made the choice as often as I possibly could to focus on myself.

In my mind, I fantasized about his healing. I wondered what his rock bottom would look like and if I would get the phone call informing me of his epiphany—the one that said, "I understand you, I am sorry, and I will work my entire life if I have to to regain your trust."

If I let my guard down, my mind ambushed me with so many scenarios that I found myself exhausted from traveling through all of the possibilities. I felt the consistent pull of God telling me that I was focusing too much on the problem. I got the sense that the Holy Spirit was trying to give me joy through the journey, but as long as I focused on the problem, I would miss out. Layer by layer, I tore my attention away from my relationship with Stephen and focused on enjoying my kids. Parenting was certainly difficult during this time as I adjusted to parenting alone, but the unique cuteness in my preschool children was too precious to miss. I didn't want to miss any more of it, so I focused and refocused on my kids. I enjoyed them and played with them and intentionally engaged them in conversation. I felt so much joy and gratitude for these little people that God had entrusted to me. The joy that radiated off of their little faces grew the joy within me and served as a nice break from my broken marriage.

Focusing on my children sustained me in my uncertainty for quite a long time, but every woman has her limit. As time went on, I became less and less OK with the in-between, and eventually I knew that it was time to make a decision. I continued to feel more capable as I studied to understand sexual addiction. I still felt crushed when I would catch Stephen lying to me or detect his gaslighting, but instead of dwelling on the disappointment and all the what-if scenarios, I focused on one day at a time. I had begun to realize how much of the hope I had felt came from the books I was reading. I projected their success stories onto my own. I was hanging on to the progress that the husbands in these books were making. So I made conscious choices to analyze and evaluate Stephen's behavior specifically instead of getting wrapped up in other people's stories and all of the emotion of his promises. Each time I succeeded, I was able to focus on what was happening in a more objective way.

As I continued to study addiction and sexually compulsive behavior, I started to put some of the puzzle pieces together. Stephen hadn't sorted out his own trauma, so he had only a limited ability to provide me with the resources I needed to deepen my understanding of what was going on with him. I knew I might never be able to put all the pieces together, but I felt comforted as I put his behavior into context. I learned how the brain works and what it takes for someone to change their mind or their behavior. These golden nuggets of information confirmed that his behavior wasn't about me not being enough.

After my curiosity was satisfied, I shifted my concentration to me. At this crossroads, I realized that no one would blame me if I demonized my husband and blamed every dysfunction of our marriage on his behavior, but in reality, that wasn't true. I began to accept that I had played a role in the breakdown of our relationship. I braved my own self-discovery and faced my own shortcomings in order to grow and focus on the only person I could control: myself.

I had justified my perfectionism by pointing to all of the praise I got for it. It had allowed me to catch the attention of my teachers and bosses. I'd tingled with delight at their compliments about my work. I paid no mind to the hours or days that I would spend obsessing over every detail, the tears I would shed when I made the slightest error, or the speed with which the delight I felt from the compliments would be choked out by all of the thoughts I would have of ways I could have made the project even better. Perfectionism did not allow me to forgive myself for being human or to extend forgiveness to others for their humanity. I recalled a performance review I had gotten from work a couple of years before. I remember my boss having delicately approached the subject by telling me that I might be expecting too much from my subordinates. I'd been baffled. Had he really criticized me for having high standards and expecting people to do their jobs correctly? All this time later, I finally realized what my boss had meant.

I made a choice not to let anyone else's actions determine my happiness. I had my own addiction to praise, and I felt like I had to perform to get it. Dealing with my own issues caused me another kind of pain. While the pain was difficult to categorize, it felt different than the pain I felt as a betrayed spouse. This pain felt productive. As my understanding of myself fell together, I felt powerful and proud of myself and made progress in my growth. It felt like the soreness you feel after a good workout. It is painful, but the more consistently you exercise, the more muscle you build. I became stronger and more pain tolerant over time. As I dove into myself with brutal honesty and open-mindedness, I was empowered to accept myself and not depend on the praise of others to feel validated. I set healthy boundaries and changed my own behavior. My responses evolved from coming out of a place of dependence to coming out of a place of independence.

As I grew personally, I realized my worth was greater than I'd thought and not based on what I could do for someone else. I started to believe that I was more than a clean house and a home-cooked meal. I realized I was more than what I looked like on the outside and how well I could hide my insecurities in front of others. I deserved the same respect as every other God-created human being, and I didn't have to live in a constant state of sacrifice. In short, I started to love myself.

Who knows what others thought? I imagine some were shocked because they had never heard the word *no* come out of my mouth. Some may have been surprised that I stopped avoiding them and just told them how I felt and what I needed. The women who were walking beside me on my journey were certainly proud of my progress. Regardless of what others thought, I felt more grounded and less exhausted. The life returned to my eyes. The time I spent with others had a better quality to it. If I did decide to serve, my service was out of a true desire to help instead of a good ole sense of obligation. I began to love out of freedom. I stopped doing things for others so that they would love me and instead rested in my innate value with the assurance that if my friends were true friends, they would still love me even if I said no sometimes. I also dealt with the fact that there would be loss and that there would be times that people were angry with me. I stopped apologizing for my imperfections and making excuses for my *nos*. I stopped trying to anticipate others' feelings and accommodate them in order to fix the negative feeling that they *might* have.

I didn't stop cold turkey, but every success further deprogrammed thirty-five years of codependency and reinforced my new perspective that allowed me to be responsible for myself and let others be responsible for themselves.

Stephen came to visit us for Memorial Day weekend. He had been kind but not forthcoming. We took the kids down to the river and splashed around. We buried our toes in the sand, caught minnows, and raced up and down the shallow bank of the waters, splashing each other with every pound of our feet. Stephen and I sat on a blanket and marveled at how our kids had grown. We had a great weekend, and the kids loved seeing him. Until that point, the kids had been under the impression that we were on vacation, though I will admit my eldest had caught on that we were staying with Grandma and Grandpa for a long time. I knew it was time to have a conversation with the kids. Stephen and I sat down with them together at bedtime.

"Hey, boys. Come sit over here with us. Mommy and Daddy need to talk to you about something important," I said. "Mommy and Daddy have made some mistakes in our marriage. We will be living in different houses until we know if we can fix those mistakes or not. If we cannot fix the mistakes, then we will always live in separate houses."

"It's OK, Mommy," my four-year-old son chimed in. "You can forgive each other, and then we can all live together, because you aren't making the mistakes anymore."

"Aw, thank you for that, sweetie," I responded. "The mistakes that we have made are big mistakes. You know how when you do a small wrong, there is a small consequence, but when you do a big wrong, then there is a big consequence. This is a big consequence."

"I want to go back to our new house with Daddy," my four-year-old said.

"Daddy has to go to work every day, sweetie, so you are going to stay here with me."

"Oh, I know," he said with a smile. "I have a great idea! Me and brother can just go to work with Daddy!"

"I'd love to have you come with me to work," Stephen said, "but my work doesn't allow kids to come. So you are going to stay here with Mom."

"Let me tell you guys," I interjected, "we will always be family. I will always be your mom and Dad will always be your dad. The mistakes we made have nothing to do with you or your brother. Our love for you is so big, and that is never going to change."

My eldest seemed to be satisfied with that answer. He asked if Stephen would lay with him as he fell asleep.

After the kids fell asleep, Stephen and I sat down to talk about divorce.

"I get that this is hard," I said. "I am giving you an out. If this twelve-step program is too hard or if it is just easier for you to move on, just let me know, and I will begin the process of filing the paperwork for divorce."

My newfound self-worth gave me the courage I needed to set my requirements and the reassurance that I would be OK no matter his response.

"I would rather you let me go than to continue to string me along," I said.

"That is not what I want," he replied. "I still want things to work out with us."

"If that is the case," I told him, "I need you to commit to taking a polygraph anytime I request."

His eyes rolled into irritation. "You are just sticking with the polygraph because that is what the therapist told you to do."

"You're right," I said, defending myself. "I would never have thought of the polygraph on my own. I don't want you to take them because I just like to follow the rules. I am asking you to take them because there is no other way that I can imagine staying with you. You have broken my trust over and over so many times that I can't trust your word right now unless it is confirmed by a test."

He sat and stared at me for a minute. "I don't know if I can agree to that. You don't understand. It is an awful experience."

"I understand that. I am sure that it is. You certainly don't have to commit to the polygraphs if it is too uncomfortable for you. I can understand why you wouldn't want to put yourself through that process over and over. If you choose not to, we can't be together, but I will be OK with whatever decision you make."

He sat in silence. There was nothing more he had to say, so I prepared for our inevitable divorce.

We said our goodbyes that weekend. The kids and I stood in the driveway waving to him as he drove away. When his car vanished down the street, we turned to go back inside the house. As I walked toward the front door, I took a deep breath, and then I crossed the threshold as a single mom.

Questions for Reflection

⇨ How does your spouse respond to your needs?

⇨ Is he accommodating or hesitant?

⇨ Is he taking responsibility for his own recovery, or do you feel like you have to push him?

My Prayer for You

Righteous Father, You created both my friend and her spouse. You know their backgrounds and how they are wired. Lord, we know that there is no rival, no stronghold, that is greater than Your power. We also acknowledge that we must be willing to be transformed by Your power. I pray for the willingness of my friend and her spouse to do whatever it takes to recover. Give my friend the discernment to know if her spouse is showing that willingness. Open her eyes to the truth, no matter where it takes her.

Hope

Hope, you are my enemy,
Hiding in the shadows
To startle me when I least expect it.

With you comes confusion,
A mix of feelings too complex to describe.

With you comes disappointment,
As you trick me into changing my
Expectations only to fall again.

I am angry at you!
And all that you stand for.
The way you make me live in
A fantasy that will never be real.

Hope, you are not welcome
Here in the land of sorrow.
What little of you there is left
Can find another victim of your lies.

Should I Stay, or Should I Go?

As MUCH AS I TRIED TO THINK OF MYSELF AS A SINGLE MOM, I paced back and forth, wavering between staying and waiting for more progress or giving up. I still felt so confused. I didn't want to make a decision as big as filing for divorce while not feeling completely secure in my decision. My brother advised me that if I didn't know which way to go, I should continue standing still. I agreed.

I started asking myself what I would and would not tolerate. I believed that I had the capacity to walk with Stephen through his addiction. I believed I had the capacity to hear his struggle with lust and support him in using healthier coping mechanisms. What I could not tolerate was lying. I felt that if Stephen were transparent with me, I could be supportive, but I wasn't willing to be left in the dark anymore.

As I felt more secure in my own worth, I more readily saw Stephen as a man in bondage that had originated and now grew with so many complexities and nuances. He still believed lies that ensnared him in addiction, but he was no less a child of God—a God who loved him dearly and longed to love him through his areas of brokenness that needed to be restored.

While God had the capacity to love Stephen unconditionally, I wrote down a list of conditions that I needed to be met before I would able to move on with him:

Stephen must break his psychological dependency on sex and basketball.

It seemed as if he was not seeing prostitutes any longer, but I was unsure of how indulgent he had been on porn and masturbation. Stephen found his significance and identity in his athletic ability. He played basketball several times a week, but I knew that if I were to return, he would need to cut his playing way down in order to fulfill his responsibilities as a dad and husband.

I needed Stephen to make me a priority.

I had poured out my heart to Stephen on several occasions without his being moved by my emotions. He came across as stoic and cold, not caring about my feelings or wounds. He had chosen not to complete the therapeutic exercises of checking in with me regularly about his progress or slips, and he had chosen not to schedule a polygraph.

Stephen needed to have the ability to cultivate and maintain deep, authentic relationships.

I had begun to notice that while Stephen had a ton of acquaintances, he did not have many (if any) close friends. He had not reported having visited with anyone about accountability in months. The frequency with which he visited the therapist had lessened and become random. He had distanced himself from the men in our Bible-study group who had tried to help him be accountable to his program. I was not able to recall the last time that I had seen him be vulnerable with me, and he was still blaming others without taking responsibility for the demise of those relationships with members of our Bible-study group. He continued to blame his lack of communication on an inability to talk effectively on the phone.

Stephen should be initiating and maintaining therapy, mentoring, and accountability regularly.

He had not given me any indication that he had accountability or mentoring in place, and his visits to therapy were becoming drastically less frequent.

I needed to see evidence that Stephen's self-centeredness was gone.

At that time, Stephen's feelings gave him a reason to dismiss my feelings. He continued to befriend and spend his time with people who felt unsafe to me. I didn't know them, but I knew that he had been with them when he had left with another woman, so I felt confident that they were not keeping him accountable. More to the point, I assumed that they had no idea of the full story of our separation. He had increased the frequency of his basketball playing but not his recovery-group or therapy visits. He had chosen not to complete another polygraph because it made him feel uncomfortable.

I needed to see evidence of Stephen's desire for spiritual growth.

He had not mentioned anything to me about regularly attending church. He'd chosen not to attend our Bible study any longer. I followed him on the YouVersion Bible app on our phones, but his devotional activity was sporadic at best. He never mentioned anything he was reading or studying to further his spiritual growth in our conversations.

I needed Stephen to consider how his actions would affect me.

Basketball had become a trigger for me. I felt like he had chosen basketball over me for quite some time, yet he had now increased his playing significantly, arguing that he could not just stay home. He could have gone to meetings or spent his time in many other ways. I had asked him to take another polygraph, but he had yet to get back with me about whether he was willing to schedule an appointment or to ask me what questions I wanted to be answered. I was thankful that he had made the long drive to my hometown. It was helpful for me not to have to drive seven hours with the boys, but part of me felt skeptical about his travels. It might have been convenient for him to travel out of town so that he could keep his two lives separate. He called frequently unless we talked about something serious; then he would go silent for days.

When I confronted him directly, he told me that he attended his twelve-step group and read his recovery book. He said he worked on doing self-reflection and maintained some level of therapy. I felt naive for holding out, waiting for him to change. As I prayed, I felt like God had not released me from this relationship. I felt timid hope and agony at the same time.

The Holy Spirit spoke to me and said, "Blessed child, I love you. Find your security in Me. I will protect you and sustain you. It is not time yet to give up. Love him. Keep your limits to feel safe, but love him. Do not let that bitter root grow up inside you. Forgive him. Forgive his brokenness and his incapability to give you what you need. It is not that he doesn't want to. He feels defeated and doesn't know how. That doesn't mean you settle, but it does mean that your worth is not dictated by his limitations. His choices don't mean that you are not valued. It means he is really broken. It will take time to rebuild. Just enjoy life. Don't let the enemy get a foothold. Find joy in the everyday. There is so much of it that I want to give you. Rest, child. Stop looking for your husband to fulfill that desire for significance. Stop looking for significance in others. You are significant because you are Mine. Your life has a purpose. You cannot even fathom the good I am doing through this situation. Focus on your life and just keep listening. I will tell you to move when it is time. It's not time to go back. There is still so much I have to teach you. I love you."

I had dreams that Stephen would grovel at my feet and ask for my forgiveness. He would pull me close, look into my eyes, and tell me that he was committed to beating his addiction so that we could be together and that I was worth changing for. In reality, time after time, my attempts to connect were met with defensiveness, vague speak, and gaslighting.

I trained myself to look at his actions instead of listening to his words. After my discovery, he had started going to a support group. He attended therapy. What I realized, though, was that if he took the steps of recovery for me, it wouldn't last. I noticed that since I had left, he had stopped doing all the things that he had done for me initially. I wasn't there to pressure him, so he'd stopped. The responsibility of his sobriety weighed more than I could carry.

Furthermore, my presence had not kept Stephen from cheating on me. While I was driven by guilt, he was driven by addiction. He would find a way to justify his actions. Stephen's negative feelings gave him permission to hurt me. He knew how much it would hurt me if he went back to the massage parlors, but when he was angry or hurt, he did it anyway, because it made him feel better at that moment.

I laid down the illusion of controlling his addiction. I had come to learn that God loves us in freedom. God has His own boundaries of things He will and won't tolerate. He does not coerce us into love. He does not guilt us into action. He invites us into His family and into the freedom of His love, but He allows us to say no. Saying no does not come without consequences, but He doesn't make us have a relationship with Him. That idea changed how I looked at my marriage. I had tried to control my husband and his actions by consistently communicating my disappointments, trying to guilt him into treating me how I wanted to be treated. What I found out was that the guilt only exacerbated the shame that comes along with addiction. But in my effort to try not to make him feel ashamed, I overcorrected and tolerated things that I was uncomfortable with. I didn't want to ask him too many questions. I let him avoid the topic while I was left in the dark. I didn't know what he was doing or how he was doing. I didn't know anything about his recovery. I didn't know how to balance letting him work his own recovery and not enabling secrecy and avoidance.

Stephen didn't volunteer information about his recovery. I told him that anything he could tell me about his recovery would help to rebuild trust between us, but I chose not to push questions. The lack of information made me hold tighter to my faith in Christ. For all I knew, he was seeing prostitutes daily, or maybe he was religiously attending recovery meetings. I just didn't know.

Once we are bonded to another person, it is not natural for us to detach. It took me a great amount of mental discipline to intentionally detach emotionally for my own well-being. I remember asking the therapist if it was possible to detach too much to the point where I would never want to be with him again. What if he was recovering and I wasn't able to reattach myself? She assured me that I would be able to reattach with the rebuilding of trust between us, but it would take concrete actions on his part, since he had continued to lie to me for so long.

My detachment turned into quiet freedom. My approach changed. I stated what I needed and did not plead or beg. I focused on the conversation and identified when it got off track. I stuck to my needs, and then, most importantly, I continued to watch his actions. I vowed to stay separated until I felt safe enough to return. The physical distance made it difficult for him to continue to manipulate me. He could no longer read my face and my body language to determine what I wanted to hear. I made the choice to start living and to start building a life where I could ensure that I would be OK with or without him as I waited to see if he would choose recovery.

The month of June began, and Stephen had not called since his Memorial Day visit. I was standing in my kitchen over a frying pan full of chicken and vegetables when the phone finally rang.

"I want you back. I want us to be a family. I will do anything," he declared.

I had waited for nine months to hear those words. I stopped cooking lunch and shut myself into the bedroom to hear him out. He proceeded to blurt out further confessions of sexual misconduct—to catch me up, I suppose.

He said, "The last time I watched porn was a week ago, and the last time I went to a massage parlor was three weeks ago. I am so sorry. I am willing to do the polygraph."

He was speaking quickly, as if to blurt everything out before he chickened out. Emotionally whiplashed, I managed to stammer out an "OK …"

"I have to go, but I will call you later," he said.

I sat in my chair, stunned but with a reserved hope. I didn't jump for joy. There was no giddy smile, just a quiet light, a wish for this time to be real.

He called me later that afternoon and surprised me with polygraph results.

"I passed," he said. "Everything came out truthful."

I felt confused and reluctantly happy about it. Stephen seemed ecstatic about the results, so I felt like I should too, but something didn't sit right. I had questions—questions that I felt like I should have had the opportunity to ask *before* he went to get a polygraph. The polygraph results did indicate that he had not had sex with another woman in our bed. I was surprised by that, honestly, but at least I could cross it off the list of my many triggers.

The following day, I wanted to clarify how he had paid for the massage parlors, because I had not seen any more withdrawals from the account. He returned my text with vague responses. My gut told me that he was hiding something. I wanted so desperately for our story to be one of redemption and reconciliation, but there I was feeling skeptical again. He answered me but not with actual facts. I felt dumb and pushy, but I continued to ask follow-up questions, because I didn't understand. Finally, he told me that he had used his personal credit card, and I wondered exactly how much more debt he had accrued.

Ten days later, I lay awake with confusion. I seemed to hold my breath, waiting to see if Stephen was sincere and if his words would actually hold true this time. He continued to tell me that he was all in and ready to do the work it took to repair our relationship, but true to form, my gut wrenched. I was skeptical, knowing deep down that his promises were unlikely to be fulfilled. I feared his manipulation and his lies. I doubted my ability to see through him, since he had fooled me for so long. My anxiety started to manifest physically. My throat hurt, my eyes turned red and dry, my head and back ached, and my hands throbbed with constant dull pain. For several nights, my racing mind kept me from sleeping. I spent my days tired, confused, and scared.

As I prayed, I felt God reassure me that I would get through this. He reminded me of His presence and said that He would walk me step by step through every decision that I needed to make. He reminded me to stop trying to control my husband, to let him initiate and lead.

During my prayer, I heard the Holy Spirit say so clearly, "In two months, you will see significant change. Your soul will be at rest … at death." I shuttered every time I heard "death." I had not had the courage to write it down in my journals until that night. The first time I'd felt a sense of death and darkness was four months prior.

I'd tried to shake the thought. I'd questioned God regularly, asking if I had heard Him correctly. I'd tried to ignore the thought when it came to mind, but the timing had been so specific. In February, I'd gotten the sense that death would happen in six months. Each time it had come to mind, it had seemed as if the timer was counting down. My heart palpated as I wondered what kind of death I would deal with. Would Stephen physically die? Would this be a spiritual death? Would this be the death of our relationship? I would find out soon enough, but there was still more roller coaster to ride in the meantime.

The intruding thoughts of death scared me. I decided it was better to avoid them at all costs, which meant avoiding prayer for the next month. I fell right back into a pattern of putting hope in Stephen and his recovery. As long as he said the right things, I seemed to be fine, but I knew that until I was physically with him again, I could not know for sure what was going on with him. I decided that I would move back in with him in October if things continued to go well and if he passed another polygraph that included my questions. A nagging feeling of uncertainty and doubt loomed over me. Unsurprisingly, stress manifested in my face, in my voice, and in my actions. I became increasingly irritable as I processed my disappointment and confusion.

I wanted to be excited that Stephen was finally ready to recover, but I had lost count of his declarations about his willingness to change. I was irritated that his progress was so slow. Shouldn't he be farther along after ten months? Then feelings of guilt crept in. What did I expect? This addiction had originated in childhood trauma and had been just shy of thirty years in the making. It also made sense to me that thirty years of struggle would not be erased in one year. I analyzed over and over and made myself sick trying to figure out what was happening.

On July 12, I sat in my closet on the phone with Stephen. The conversation quickly turned into an argument. It was one of many of the same. I don't recall exactly what it was about, but I would presume it went something along the lines of him hiding or not communicating something to me resulting in me getting triggered. I likely confronted him about it, and he countered with one of his favorite responses: excuses, vague speech where he uses a lot of words but in reality explains nothing, or a countermove that deflected the attention off of him and onto me and my over-emotional reaction. Then, there was silence. No calls. No texts.

My anxiety soared through the roof. How could he just disappear? What was he doing? I attempted to escape my problems by taking the weekend to visit my brother. Instead of escaping my problems, I dived into them head deep with a bottle of chardonnay and a toilet bowl. I slept that bad idea off and needed a new plan. I strategized my next escape and traveled with my family to the lake. Unfortunately, I forgot to leave my problems at home. Just as I would start to relax and enjoy the sun and the water, I would remember that Stephen still hadn't called. I prayed short little prayers here and there, and I got a strong sense that I should not call him. God urged me over and over not to try to control the situation, as much as I wanted to. I thought that talking to him would make the anxiety go away. If I just called, I wouldn't have to feel like this anymore. If I called, maybe I would stop making up stories in my head, imagining the worst. My experience should have taught me that this strategy rarely worked, but my pain was deep, so practicing self-control seemed as difficult as lifting a car.

Stephen finally called while I was at the lake. It had been nine days since I had heard from him. I stepped into my cousin's camper for privacy. He told me that he had seen the therapist and was calling to tell me that he was not good at communicating and that he didn't want to talk for hours each phone call. He continued to tell me that he felt intimidated talking to me because I spoke too well. He asked me to back off and stop interrogating him. I felt so desperate to get to know Stephen, who I had come to learn so painfully was not the man I thought I'd married. I only asked questions because he told me nothing. When we hung up the phone, my hope and energy were depleted. The conversation had only confused me more as to where we stood and what was happening. The evening turned into day, and my anxiety burst through my body. I found myself convulsing with panic in my cousin's camper. My cousin stood in shock while my aunt instructed her to get me a blanket. My aunt held me close, and my voice went mute while my body became numb from the intense vibration of my limbs. My aunt gave me some water and prayed over me with such sincerity. As they left, I rested alone in the camper, knowing I could not continue this way.

I sat in my car later that afternoon talking with my support-group buddy, Chloe. I needed to talk to someone who understood the stakes. She helped me process the situation, and after talking with her, I decided that I was going to call Stephen and give him my final terms.

I dialed Stephen's number. He answered and immediately told me he was in the middle of a child's birthday party, but I couldn't stop the verbal vomit from spewing out of my mouth.

"I don't want to hide or blindside you. I am just letting you know that if things don't improve significantly between us by my birthday, I plan on filing for divorce." My birthday would come two months from that day, nine months after our separation, and a full year since I had discovered his secret life.

"What are you talking about? I am doing what I need to do," he blurted.

"The thing is that I have no idea what you are doing because you are not telling me. I can't feel safe if I don't know what is going on. Your level of transparency with me needs to change. So regardless of what you are doing, if I don't feel safe with you, I am going to file."

We continued back and forth for a few minutes. I hated this same old fight. By the end of the conversation, he seemed to have convinced himself that he wanted me and that he would work his hardest for us to be a family.

"OK, I'm ready," he said as if he was pumping himself up for a basketball game. "I'm all in. I am going all in."

"If that is how you feel, then I need absolute transparency with your technology, finances, and whereabouts, and I will need periodic polygraphs to help verify that you are telling the truth," I replied.

As if he were calling a Hail Mary, he replied back, "I am ready to give all I have for us."

The days and weeks following, Stephen called and texted more. I felt torn as I reflected on our relationship. Stephen was my friend whom I loved so deeply. When he wasn't hurting me, I adored him and loved spending time with him. He made me laugh. I loved his silliness and his affection. I loved how he towered over me and made me feel delicate and feminine. I loved how everyone he met instantly seemed to love him and how he never seemed to judge a book by its cover. I loved seeing his giant hands rock our tiny baby boys and how my heart would still skip a beat when he called me beautiful. How could I reconcile that man with the one I knew today? This man lied to me. This man put me in physical danger. He knowingly deceived me for so many years. He seemed incapable of a true apology. Asking him to have an authentic and vulnerable conversation with me was like asking him to move mountains. We'd had an epic romance, one that addiction had stolen from us, and I feared we would never fully get it back.

As I prayed, God was still urging me to give Him control. I wasn't exactly mad at God, but I certainly felt impatient with Him. I asked God continuously what would happen with us, but He steadfastly gave me one direction at a time.

As I waited for directions, I kept focusing on self-care and spirituality. I reminded myself of my worth and stopped reinforcing lies I had believed with twisted scripture. I had taken the scripture that speaks of imitators of Christ to mean that I was supposed to be Christ. Talk about an impossible standard! Here I was reading scripture about Jesus and trying to be Jesus in my faulty humanity. As a bonus, I also tried to be the Holy Spirit to others and convince them of what they should do, especially Stephen. Instead of leading them to the Holy Spirit, I just took them on frequent guilt trips. After all, the false guilt and disappointment I thought God felt for me had driven me for a long time.

This journey helped me learn that God was not annoyed with me or disappointed in me. He genuinely loved me and yearned for me to live the abundant life He promised. I love the analogy that likens the Holy Spirit to the wind. You can't see it, but you see the effects the wind has on everything it touches. As I took a leap of faith and stopped to listen, The Holy Spirit was generous with His encouragement and reassurance. He paced me, and as I honored His timing, He took care of me and healed my heart with His presence throughout my progress.

I received God's love and belonging and started to give myself a break. Maybe I really didn't need to be perfect to be loved. I was not meant to carry the burdens of the world. I was a beautiful human, plagued with the human condition of needing food and rest. My body was not a machine, even though I expected it to run like one most of the time. I had to take care of myself if I wanted to take care of others. I had to stop enabling those I loved the most by saving them and preventing them from growing. My world would not fall apart if I failed to control every aspect.

I continued to get to know myself. Through spirituality and self-care, I learned about myself and my needs. I learned to roll with the punches as my confidence grew in God, knowing He has the power to take me through anything that comes my way. One day at a time, my life became more manageable, and my skin became thicker with the protection of my identity as a beloved child of God.

Questions for Reflection

⇨ Take a moment and ask God how He sees you. What is He saying?

⇨ What self-care strategies can you realistically commit to on a regular basis?

⇨ Battle any fears of inadequacy by reciting Godly affirmations. For more information, refer to the appendix.

My Prayer for You

Holy Father, it's easy to not feel like we're enough. Often we feel like we must prove to others that we are worthy of love. Remind my friend, in this moment, that she is loved for who she is and not what she does. Remind her that she has nothing to prove. Fullfill your promises, Lord, not to leave her. Be her rest and refuge. Continue to show up in her times of trouble. Help her believe You when You say she is strong and worthy. She is Your beloved daughter. Help her love herself as You have loved her. Let her see herself how You see her. Amen.

The Beginning
of the End

*A*UGUST BEGAN, AND THE DAYS CAME AND WENT. MY
strength dipped as my mind became preoccupied.
My body cringed with unrest, desperate to know the
next move. I felt as though I had waited for so long in anticipation
of what God would have me do. I was willing to be obedient,
but my spirit was growing more tired and weak by the day. As I
prayed, the Holy Spirit reminded me to trust Him, and reminded
me that I would have to risk opening myself up to find the truth.
He reassured me that He would be there with me the entire way
as my refuge and told me that the direction I needed to take would
become clear at the end of the month.

The weekend of August 19, Stephen came to visit. That
weekend, like many other times before, I felt a sense of wholeness
having our entire family together. I loved watching the kids play
with their dad and then cuddle up next to him to fall asleep after
a full day of activity. Kacey Musgraves played in the background:

I try to sleep; I just lie here awake.
I've stopped counting sheep; now I just count the days
Till you're back in this bed that I remake every time.
And if they ask, I'll say I'm fine.

I saw a tear roll down Stephen's cheek. I wiped his tears and gave him a hug. We sat on the couch and found tickets to a concert of a band I loved, so I decided to follow him back to the city to attend the concert. Stephen and I had already talked about my plans to contingently move back in October, and we decided to slowly date again as a way to connect after being separated. I packed up our bags to head to the city on Sunday morning after church. The kids rode with their dad, and I followed behind in my car. I took deep, calming breaths inside my car. A break from the kids felt relaxing. I listened to the music and books I wanted to. It was nice to get away from cartoons for a moment. One hour into our travels, my car totally malfunctioned. Steam burst from the hood and traveled back toward the rear of the car. I slowed down and pulled over to the shoulder of the road. I called Stephen who was travelling ahead of me to tell him what happened. He slowed down and did a U-turn back toward me. He pulled over to the side of the road beside me. We looked under the hood in ignorance and tried to start the car again, but it would not turn over. After a couple of tries, I put the car in neutral and Stephen pushed it farther over into the grass, far out of the way of traffic. I unloaded the luggage in my car and squeezed into his. We all rode together back to the city.

When we arrived, we settled into the house. Stephen encouraged me to search the house and do what I needed to feel safe. I made my rounds, and he played with the kids outside. I looked out the window from the second floor, watching them. I stared at my fairy tale, Stephen playing with our boys running and laughing. I stood in the master bedroom of my dream house—four bedrooms, big but not too big, with a giant backyard in which to run and play. It was a safe neighborhood that was just old enough to have character but not so old that the house lacked the advances I needed. I had a grocery store, a pharmacy, a clinic, and an elementary school within a few blocks. The house stood less than ten minutes away from the homes of three different close friends, as well as my church that I loved and whose members had grown to feel like family. I wished desperately to come back to this place that felt so much like home.

Stephen and I still slept in different rooms. I stood firm with that boundary to stay separate until I got results from another planned polygraph that included the questions I needed answered. As we passed each other in the hall, Stephen reached out to give me a hug. I hugged him back and slightly pulled away, still embracing him. I looked deeply into his eyes.

"Do you promise you are abstaining?" I asked quietly.

"I am," he responded reassuringly.

"What is your abstinence date, again?" I questioned.

He looked away from me, irritated. "I don't know the exact date. I am not focusing on the past and on the dates but on the future."

Disappointed again in his answer, I reminded him, "When you last confessed to me, you told me that the first of May was the last time you had been to a massage parlor. Is that still correct?"

"Yes," he assured me.

The next day, Stephen went to work. The boys and I were somewhat stranded, since my car hadn't made it to the city. Some friends came to hang out with us, and we ended up having a wonderful day. That evening, Stephen returned home. We ate dinner as a family and spent some quality time together.

I had arranged to see my dear friend from work, Reba, on Wednesday, August 23. I asked Stephen if I could keep the car so I could go visit her. He agreed and hitched a ride with a friend to work so that I could use his car. The boys and I got ready for our adventures that morning and headed out to see my friend.

I pulled up into the parking lot of my former office building. The customer parking lot was full, so I pulled around to the employee parking in the back. I called Reba and asked if she could come and let us in the locked back door. She gladly came out and helped me unload my small kids and my mom gear (snacks, diapers, toys, etc.). She flashed her employee badge against the back door lock. There I entered my former workplace ... and the truth for which I had been searching.

My Prayer for You

All-knowing Father, You are the only one who knows our innermost thoughts and motivations. You are the only one who knows the full truth. I pray that in Your perfect timing, You would bring the darkness into the light. I pray that my friend is able to receive the truth, however it is presented. We acknowledge Your sovereignty and how You are constantly working in the background. Bring all of the pieces together to reveal the truth my friend needs to hear. Give her the courage and the fortitude to withstand the suffering that is often accompanied with revelation.

The Moment it All Became Clear

EBA ESCORTED THE BOYS AND ME THROUGH THE BACK hallway toward my old office. I had visited several times since I'd resigned and had already met my replacement, Jessica. During my previous visits, I'd rarely given her more than an acknowledging wave as I crossed the hallway to visit my former work team. It wasn't anything personal; I just didn't have a relationship with her, since we had not worked together. Reba, oddly, walked into Jessica's office to say hi and to show her that I was visiting. We exchanged a few pleasantries and then moved on toward the offices of my former team.

I was catching up with another former co-worker, Hazel, when Jessica entered the room and told me that she had gotten a call for me on her office phone, my former office phone. The group of us talking all thought this to be strange, since it had been almost a year and a half since I'd been employed. She handed me a post-it with a phone number and the name Christ Walker written on it. I joked that if Christ was calling me, I better pay attention to it. Little did I know in that moment that this was actually Jesus's way of getting my attention.

Reba escorted me and my kids back to her office. We closed the door, got the kids settled, and started our own catch-up session. Reba's phone rang. It was Hazel calling. As they talked, I recalled how Reba had confessed to me a few months ago that she'd let it slip to Hazel that Stephen and I were separated. Reba was so apologetic, because keeping confidentiality was important to her and she knew how important it was for me to keep my situation out of the office rumor-mill.

Reba hung up the phone and turned to me with a look of quiet sadness and strength. She spoke in code to protect my children's little ears. She handed me the post-it with the information about the phone call for me.

"The person who called your old office called from a massage parlor looking for Stephen."

I just stared at her in shock and embarrassment.

"I don't know what this means," she said, "but I am sure that it should not be ignored. Why don't you step outside and make a phone call?"

I stepped outside and called Stephen.

"Infinite Massage just called my old office phone looking for you," I said, seething.

He fumbled with his answer. "Why would they call your old office?" he asked.

"I don't know. You tell me."

"Maybe they have been calling to get me to come back but were not able to reach me, so they called you?"

"How do they even know who I am or where I used to work?" I shouted. "Do you know how embarrassing this is?"

"I don't know. I'm sorry, but really, shouldn't that show you that I haven't been? Otherwise, they would have just called me," he reasoned.

"Have you ever been to Infinite Massage?" I asked.

"I don't know … I can't remember … maybe."

"What do you mean you don't know? Have you ever been to Walmart? It's not a hard question."

"Come on, now. What do you want me to do? Do you want me to check into it and call you back?"

My breathing slowed, and my eyes glazed over as I gazed out into the parking lot sitting on the steps of the office building. At that moment, I realized that it didn't matter what he said or what he did.

"You know, I don't want you to check into it actually. Why would I believe the person who has lied to me the most? Even if you do everything correctly from this point on, there has been too much deception. I just cannot trust you."

"Wow," he said bewildered.

We said our goodbyes, and I walked back into Reba's office. I felt completely crushed. I described my phone conversation to her. She responded with a confused look.

"Why did you call your husband? I thought you were calling the massage parlor."

"Am I just supposed to pretend that I am him?" I asked nervously.

"The parlor was intentionally calling you. They are trying to get a message to Stephen. Just call back and tell them that you received their message."

I nodded as tears welled in my eyes.

"I will take the boys to lunch with me," she continued. "Go home and call, and I will meet you at your house in an hour."

I agreed and headed home.

When I arrived home, I prayed for the strength to keep my cool during the phone call. I dialed the number from the yellow post-it and waited as the phone rang.

Voicemail.

Panicked about whether or not to leave a message, I paused and then began to speak.

"This is Kristen; I am returning your call. You can reach me at this number." I sat at the kitchen table, my leg uncontrollably shaking. I decided that I needed to eat something, even if I wasn't hungry. I forced myself to make a sandwich and sat to eat with my mind racing as to what I should do next. All of a sudden, my phone rang. It was the parlor.

"Hello. This is Kristen," I said.

A woman's voice answered on the other end. She spoke fast and hostilely.

"I need you to tell your husband that I am going to sue him for theft of service," she yelled. "He charged three separate massage appointments on his credit card and then canceled them through the bank. He is not getting away with this!"

"Wow, OK," I responded with superhuman restraint.

"I don't know if you know this, but our business is not one that you could find on the internet, if you know what I mean. We are a referral-only business."

I could practically hear her wink over the phone as she said it, trying to tell me that her business employed prostitutes without incriminating herself.

"Oh, OK," I responded.

She continued to speak, "And let me tell you, I have evidence. I have video footage, text messages …"

She continued to set out her case. She had the evidence. She was telling the truth.

I calmly said to her, "I understand. Can you tell me the date of his last massage?"

She replied, "July twenty-eighth."

"OK, thank you," I replied. "I will make sure he gets the message."

Black-and-white confirmation. Stephen had assured me two days prior that his last slip had happened almost four months ago in the first week in May. Now, there was evidence that he had received services from this massage parlor just three weeks ago. Again, I had caught him in a lie. Stephen was just not willing to be honest with me.

I sat at the kitchen table in my dream house. In seven days, the calendar showed, it would be our one-year anniversary of moving into that house, a year since the chaos had started, and eleven months since I had sheepishly walked into my gynecologist's office to get a shot for the gonorrhea that my husband had given to me. I'd had enough. I had *finally* reached my limit. Through this weird, totally divine intervention, I knew the truth without a shadow of a doubt and was ready to make my choice.

Reba pulled into the driveway to drop off my kids. I had already packed our bags. I told her what had happened, and she reassured me that I was doing the right thing. As she drove off, I buckled my kids into Stephen's car and loaded our luggage. I told the kids that there was an emergency and we needed to cut our trip short and go back to our vacation home. I popped in a DVD for the kids and took one last look at the life I was leaving behind. I took a deep breath and then began the long drive back.

As I drove the long and winding roads that lead out of the city, the rain pummeled down on my windshield. The wipers raced as fast as they could back and forth across the windshield, but my view remained blurred. While the weather matched the chaos that my mind had experienced for the last year, my present mind was uncharacteristically calm and quiet. I experienced peace that surpasses understanding. I had analyzed and agonized, wondering how long was too long to wait for my family to stay together. I had hoped and doubted. My stomach and mind had ached with anxiety. I had been starved with stress. I had binged with stress. Now, though the storm raged around me, I was completely satisfied with my decision and my life.

After driving for hours, I began to tire, and my adrenaline gradually decreased. The rain had slowed to a drizzle, and I decided to call a friend of mine who lived around the halfway point of our drive. She welcomed us to stay the night and rest before continuing our travels in the morning. As I turned to head in the direction of her house, there before me, a bright and colorful rainbow arced across the sky. There before me was a picture of God's promise of protection. At that moment, I knew without a doubt that I would not only survive this life but would thrive.

Questions for Reflection

⇨ Close your eyes and ask God to show you the abundance He has promised you. What do you see?

⇨ Take a minute to just let go. Let go of all of the expectations. Let go of all of the obligations. Let go of life you'd thought you had. Surrender to the plan that God is giving you.

My Prayer for You

Mysterious Father, I pray that my friend would stop trying to understand the why and just follow Your lead. I pray that You would lead her into the abundant life that You promised her with or without her husband. Continue to guide her steps. Help her put complete trust in You as you direct her path. I pray that You would display Your love and protection of her in a mighty way.

The Aftermath

STEPHEN STARTED BLOWING UP MY PHONE WITH TEXT MESSAGES when the boys and I never came home. The service was spotty where I was, so I just texted him that we were OK but were not coming home that night. The following morning, the boys and I packed back up in the car, and I called a divorce attorney in my hometown to schedule an appointment. I waited until the paperwork was filed and then emailed Stephen about my decision. He didn't seem surprised. In fact, he wrote that he understood and then immediately asked about the car.

I travelled back to the city with my mother and the boys shortly after that to pack up my half of our belongings. When I began filling boxes with my things, halving all my possessions with Stephen, my Snow White puzzle caught my eye. It had been buried under junk, long forgotten in the chaos. I looked at it with a new determination. I was going to finish that puzzle. I would not leave it broken to eventually be thrown out with the weekly scheduled garbage pick-up. I packed it carefully and ensured that it would be protected on the long seven-hour drive back to the town where I was born.

Stephen and I had dinner with the boys on our back deck and told them that we couldn't fix our mistakes and so would permanently live in different houses. They were young and didn't grasp the gravity of the situation. They acknowledged the update and then went to play in the yard. Stephen and I sat on the deck, watching them together. I took in the breeze and the beautiful greenbelt behind our house. I listened to the boy's laughter and felt the sadness and grief behind this fairy-tale picture. The next day, Stephen and I sat in a coffee shop and had the hard conversation of negotiating the parameters for our divorce decree.

My father came to pick us up with a moving trailer a few days later. With my parents and my kids in the car, I stood alone with Stephen and gave him one final kiss goodbye. He cried as we drove away from the house. I had forgiven him for what he'd done to me. I'd acknowledged his brokenness and wished him the best.

Upon our arrival back home, I knew it was time to pull my Snow White puzzle back out. I was ready to put the pieces back together. I was tired of being broken. That puzzle became a visual symbol of my personal growth. Each time I found a piece, I celebrated. It reminded me of how God restores each broken piece of my life to create a beautiful masterpiece of His handiwork. Ephesians 2:10 (NLT) says, "For we are God's masterpiece. He has created us anew in Christ Jesus, so we can do the good things he planned for us long ago."

I'd like to tell you that we have remained friends and that we are all very mature at our family gatherings, but unfortunately, as I write this book, that's not part of our story. I tried to stay connected with Stephen as a friend after I filed, but that is a story for another time. As time went on, it got too complicated for us to have any connection beyond business with the kids. I am so fortunate to still be connected with his parents and extended family. They are a continuing blessing to me. I love them deeply and truly consider them to be my forever family. The boys remain in close contact with them, and I am daily grateful for the connection that we all share.

The boys have adjusted to their new living situation better than I could ever have imagined. They have many villages that love them immensely, and it is evident that they feel secure and safe and loved.

Final Words

S I WRITE TODAY, A LITTLE OVER TWO YEARS FROM MY discovery date, I am amazed at the difference a day makes. I remember like it was yesterday, sitting in my bed with a darkness and literal heaviness in my spirit looking up the fastest way to die. Now, after two years, tons of therapy and support-group sessions, countless hours of prayer, and a bunch of trial and error, I find myself feeling free.

My freedom doesn't come from a spiteful place. I am not trying to jump into bed with another man to prove to Stephen (and myself) that I am wanted. My freedom comes from my ability to love myself in the purest of ways, without conceit or false confidence but with grace. I embrace my imperfections. I own my anxieties. I have trained my inner voice to speak kindly and with compassion. I am happily imperfect. My freedom comes from letting go of what I thought my life should look like and embracing what it has become. I remain open to the idea of love, but I am secure enough on my own to make the wisest choices for myself and prioritize loving my kids and being an intentional mom.

Freedom is never free. Somebody pays an enormous cost

every time. My freedom wasn't free. I paid in tears, in faith, in sleepless nights, and in the hard work of recovery. I hate that it took something this big to get me to examine myself and my own issues, but I wasn't about to let this betrayal dictate the end of my story. I spent hours upon hours intentionally working to figure out where my hang-ups came from. I braved the deep dark places in my past. Now, I am stepping out in courage with the hope that the story of my journey will help you along yours.

God doesn't waste pain. He didn't cause this pain to happen to you. Sin caused this pain. God is mourning with you. He is feeling the depth of despair with you. Jesus is an empathetic Savior who experienced his own great betrayal. He will not waste your pain. Let that pain be a catalyst for change in you.

So, here's to new beginnings. I would like to leave you with a prayer. This is a prayer for each one of you who is going through or has gone through this kind of betrayal. None of us wanted this for our marriage or for our lives. I still grieve the fact that this is my story. But here we are, battle buddies together, in a club that none of us wanted to join. Let's make the most of it.

Heavenly Father, You are faithful. You have our best interests at heart. You smile with joy because of us. You love when we laugh. You are proud of us in our triumph. You also mourn with us when we mourn. Your heart breaks at our brokenness. You will not be mocked, and Your power is strong and endless. You do not sleep, and You do not rest. You fight on our behalf in the background, even when our situations look hopeless in front of us.

We lay our brokenness at Your feet, Jesus. We lay down our pain. We lay down our fears. We lay down the disappointment that these situations are part of our stories. We lay these things down, Lord. We know that You will carry them as long as we let You, as long as we don't pick them back up. We ask You, Lord, for stamina. We ask You to hold our hands through this journey. Be our hope. Give us the wisdom that You promise us—a wisdom that is plentiful and free for those of us who seek it.

I pray for clarity and patience. I pray, Lord God, for each woman who is trying to decide whether she should stay or go. I pray that You would calm her spirit enough to give her supernatural patience—not a patience that would continue to excuse abuse but a patience that would wait on Your voice.

I pray for a hunger and thirst for You. I pray that these women's prayer lives would come alive and that they can discern the voice of the Holy Spirit. I pray for Your supernatural peace in the midst of the chaos. I pray for the peace that comes with rest in Your will. I pray against the naysayers that would either tell these women to get back at their husbands by cheating on them in retaliation or tell them that they need to blindly trust their husbands and stay with them just because that is what a "good Christian woman" would do. Equip each woman with wisdom to make her own decision to walk alongside her husband in his journey of recovery or to start a life without him as her husband, equipping her to separate. Lord Jesus, we declare this day that You will not waste our pain.

We declare that You are bigger than this and that this is not the end of our stories. We pray expectantly for the mighty and victorious works You will do in our lives. We pray for the freedom that can only be experienced by owning our identities in You. In Jesus's sweet name, I pray. Amen.

Appendix

Helpful Books

Book Title	Author
Your Sexually Addicted Spouse: How Partners Can Cope and Heal	Barbara Steffens, Randye Kaye, et al.
Boundaries Updated and Expanded Edition: When to Say Yes, How to Say No To Take Control of Your Life	Dr. Henry Cloud and Dr. John Townsend
Beyond Boundaries: Learning to Trust Again in Relationships	Dr. Henry Cloud and Dr. John Townsend
Journey to Healing and Joy: A Workbook for Partners of Sexual Addicts	Marsha Means MA
L.I.F.E. Recovery Guide for Spouses: A Workbook for Living in Freedom Everyday in Sexual Wholeness and Integrity	Melissa Haas and Dr. Mark Laaser

Shattered Vows: Hope and Healing for Women Who Have Been Sexually Betrayed	Debra Laaser
Codependent No More: How to Stop Controlling Others and Start Caring for Yourself	Melody Beattie
Out of the Shadows: Understanding Sexual Addiction	Patrick J Carnes Ph.D
It's Not Supposed to Be This Way: Finding Unexpected Strength When Disappointments Leave You Shattered	Lysa TerKeurst
Choosing Forgiveness: Your Journey to Freedom	Nancy Leigh DeMoss
Braving the Wilderness: The Quest for True Belonging and the Courage to Stand Alone	Brené Brown
Rising Strong: How the Ability to Reset Transforms the Way We Live, Love, Parent, and Lead	Brené Brown
Safe People: How to Find Relationships That Are Good for You and Avoid Those That Aren't	Dr. Henry Cloud and Dr. John Townsend
Worthy of Her Trust: What You Need to Do to Rebuild Sexual Integrity and Win Her Back	Stephen Arterburn and Jason B. Martinkus
Help Her Heal: An Empathy Workbook for Sex Addicts to Help their Partners Heal	Carol Juergensen Sheets, Allan J. Katz, Chris Bordey

List of Healthy Coping Mechanisms

I love this list from Infinite Mindcare so I have included it here for you. Please remember to give yourself grace as you cope with this devastating situation. You will inevitably fall into negative coping strategies, but I encourage you to gradually work on replacing those strategies with more positive solutions.

Positive Coping Skills	Negative Coping Skills
	Diversions
• Write, draw, paint, photography • Play an instrument, sing, dance, act • Take a shower or a bath • Garden • Take a walk, or go for a drive • Watch television or a movie • Watch cute kitten videos on YouTube • Play a game • Go shopping • Clean or organize your environment • Read • Take a break or vacation	• Procrastination • Abusing drugs or alcohol • Wasting time on unimportant tasks
Social/Interpersonal (with others)	Interpersonal (With Others)
• Talk to someone you trust • Set boundaries and say "no" • Write a note to someone you care about • Be assertive • Use humor • Spend time with friends and/or family • Serve someone in need • Care for or play with a pet • Role-play challenging situations with others • Encourage others	• Blaming • Isolating/withdrawing • Mean or hostile joking • Gossiping • Criticizing others • Manipulating others • Refusing help from others • Lying to others • Sabotaging plans • Being late to appointments • Provoking violence from others • Enabling others to take advantage of you

Cognitive (Of the Mind)	Cognitive (of the Mind)
• Make a gratitude list • Brainstorm solutions • Lower your expectations of the situation • Keep an inspirational quote with you • Be flexible • Write a list of goals • Take a class • Act opposite of negative feelings • Write a list of pros and cons for decisions • Reward or pamper yourself when successful • Write a list of strengths • Accept a challenge with a positive attitude	• Denying any problem • Stubbornness/inflexibility • All or nothing/black or white thinking • Catastrophizing • Overgeneralizing
Tension Releasers	**Tension Releasers**
• Exercise or play sports • Catharsis (yelling in the bathroom, punching a punching bag) • Cry • Laugh	• Tantrums • Throwing things at people • Hitting people • Yelling at others • Destroying property • Speeding or driving recklessly
Physical	**Physical**
• Get enough sleep • Eat healthy foods • Get into a good routine • Eat a little chocolate • Limit caffeine • Deep/slow breathing	• Suicide • Self harm • Developing illnesses
Spiritual	**Intrapersonal**
• Pray or meditate • Enjoy nature • Get involved in a worthy cause	• Making fun of yourself • Self-sabotaging behaviors • Blaming yourself

Limit Setting	Indulging
• Drop some involvement • Prioritize important tasks • Use assertive communication • Schedule time for yourself	• Spending too much • Gambling • Eating too much • Setting dangerous fires • Continually crying

Author: Blake Flannery
Sourced by:
https://healdove.com/mental-health/Coping-Strategies-Skills-List-Positive-Negative-Anger-Anxiety-Depression-Copers
Found at:
https://www.infinitemindcare.com/single-post/2016/12/18/a-list-of-coping-skills-for-anger-anxiety-and-depression

Therapeutic Resources

The following are a couple of outlines I received from my therapist that I found helpful.

Weekly Check-In
Sexual Addict

1. This is a time to summarize your feelings for the week. Which feelings stand out? Also, which feelings are you experiencing right now? You may be experiencing several feelings in the moment. Take them one at a time.
2. This is the time to summarize your week's recovery. How many meetings have you attended? How many times have you contacted your accountability partner and sponsor? Did you go to individual therapy? What has been your spiritual routine? What exercise and/or step are you working on? Are you reading any recovery books, and if so what did you learn?
3. Share things that triggered you to take a second look, start to fantasize, lust or act out.
4. What did you do to overcome the above situations? Prayer, snapping your wrist, avoiding certain areas, etc.
5. Be honest about any slips or relapses that may have occurred during the week and state how long you have been sober.

Check-ins should be done the same day and time each week. This should be a permanent practice in the marriage. It is the addict's responsibility to initiate regularly and timely. This rebuilds trust and allows the spouse to stop having to play detective and interrogator. A plan should be formulated and agreed upon in advance for any unforeseen travel or periods of separation.

During this check-in, the spouse is discouraged from asking questions in order to create a safe environment to disclose information. If there are questions, try to save them for the next day. At the end of the check-in, if you are able, thank your partner for having the courage to take one more step toward a truthful marriage. Although triggers are very difficult for the spouse to hear, it gets easier with time and is much better than not knowing. It is critical that you avoid harboring secrets.

The purpose of the check-in is two-fold: To give the one struggling with a sexual addiction a safe environment to disclose his feelings, triggers, recovery work, and any slips or relapses that may have occurred AND to help the wife feel safe in the knowledge that her spouse is still in recovery and there are not any secrets. Remember the reality that every man is confronted with temptation on a daily basis. If your husband is checking in with you about this weekly, you have a much more honest relationship than most couples.

Weekly Check-In
Partner

1. This is a time to summarize your feelings for the week. Which feelings stand out? Also, which feelings are you experiencing right now? You may be experiencing several feelings in the moment. Take them one at a time.
2. This is the time to summarize your week's recovery. How many support group meetings have you attended? Did you go to individual therapy? What has been your spiritual routine? Are you reading any recovery books and if so what did you learn? If you're working a workbook, what specifically are you working on?
3. Be honest about any obsessive thoughts, feelings, or behaviors.
4. Share things that triggered overwhelming feelings, thoughts, and behaviors.

5. What did you do to overcome the above situations? (ex; prayer, stop technique, distraction strategies, time outs, imagery, grounding statements, surfing the urge.)

Check-ins should be done the same day and time each week. This should be a permanent practice in the marriage

During this check-in, the spouse is discouraged from asking questions in order to create a safe environment to disclose information. If there are questions, try to save them for the next day

Affirmations

Steps to Identify Clarification:

1. Each day, read what God says about you.
2. Verbally state out loud what God says.
3. Meditate on the truth and ask God to speak to you.
4. Write down your impressions and signification scriptures.
5. Draw a line through what you feel or think about yourself that is contrary to what God says.

The Lie	The Truth	Proof
I am unworthy/ unacceptable.	I am accepted and worthy.	Romans 15:7 Psalm 139:13-24
I feel like I am a failure, inadequate.	I am adequate.	2 Corinthians 3:5-6 Philippians 4:13
I am fearful/anxious.	I am free from fear.	Psalm 34:4,11 Timothy 1:7 1 Peter 5:7 1 John 4:18
I am a weak person.	I am strong in Christ.	Daniel 11:32 Psalm 37:39 Philippians 4
I am not smart.	I have God's wisdom.	Proverbs 2:6-7 1 Corinthians 1:30 James 1:5
I am in bondage.	I am free.	Psalm 32:7 1 Corinthians 2:17 John 8:36 Isaiah 40:9-16
I am unloved.	I am very loved.	John 15:9 Romans 8:35-39 Ephesians 2:4 Ephesians 5:1 1 John 4: 10-11

I am unwanted/I don't belong to anyone.	**I have been adopted by God and am His child.**	Romans 8:16 Galatians 1:14 Ephesians 1:5 1 John 3:2
I feel guilty.	**I am totally forgiven.**	Psalm 103: 12 Ephesians 1:7 Colossians 1:14, 20 Hebrews 10:17
I am depressed and hopeless.	**I have all the hope I need.**	Romans 15:13 Psalms 16:11, 27, 13 Psalms 31:24
This is nothing special about me.	**I have been chosen; set apart by God.**	Psalm 139 1 Corinthians 1:30 Psalm 6:11 Hebrews 10:10, 14
I am not good enough.	**I am perfect in Christ.**	Hebrew 10:14 Colossians 2:13
I am defeated.	**I am victorious.**	Romans 8:37 1 Corinthians 2:14 1 John 5:4
I have no strength.	**I have God's power, indwelt by the Holy Spirit.**	Acts 1:8 Ephesians 1:19 Ephesians 3:16 Romans 8:9-11
I feel condemned.	**I am blameless.**	Romans 8:11 1 John 3:18
I am alone.	**I am never alone.**	Hebrews 13:5 Romans 8:38-39
I have no one to take care of me.	**I am protected and safe.**	Psalms 32:7-11 Psalms 27:1-6 Psalms 41
I can't reach God.	**I have access to God.**	Ephesians 2:6 1 Peter 2:5 Matthew 6:14
I am afraid of Satan.	**I have authority over Satan.**	Colossians 1:13 1 John 4:4 Revelation 12:7-11

I have no confidence.	**I have all the confidence I need.**	Proverbs 3:26
		Hebrews 10:19
		Ephesians 3:12
		Proverbs 14:26
		Proverbs 28:1

Printed in the United States
by Baker & Taylor Publisher Services